The Long View

DONNA SINCLAIR

THE
LONG VIEW

AN ELDERWOMAN'S
BOOK OF WISDOM

Northstone

Editor: Ellen Turnbull
Cover and interior design: Verena Velten
Pre-press production: Margaret Kyle
Proofreader: Dianne Greenslade

Northstone is an imprint of Wood Lake Publishing, Inc. Wood Lake Publishing acknowledges the financial support of the Government of Canada, through the Book Publishing Industry Development Program (BPIDP) for its publishing activities. Wood Lake Publishing also acknowledges the financial support of the Province of British Columbia through the Book Publishing Tax Credit.

At Wood Lake Publishing, we practise what we publish, being guided by a concern for fairness, justice, and equal opportunity in all of our relationships with employees and customers. Wood Lake Publishing is committed to caring for the environment and all creation. Wood Lake Publishing recycles, reuses, and encourages readers to do the same. Resources are printed on 100% post-consumer recycled paper and more environmentally friendly groundwood papers (newsprint), whenever possible. A percentage of all profit is donated to charitable organizations.

Library and Archives Canada Cataloguing in Publication
Sinclair, Donna, 1943-
    The long view : an elderwoman's book of wisdom / Donna Sinclair.
ISBN 978-1-55145-595-2
    1. Older women--Prayers and devotions. 2. Aging--Religious aspects--Christianity--Meditations.
3. Devotional calendars. I. Title.
BV4580.S55 2011   242'.65   C2011-904837-X

Published by Northstone
An imprint of Wood Lake Publishing Inc.
9590 Jim Bailey Road, Kelowna, BC, Canada, V4V 1R2
www.woodlakebooks.com
250.766.2778

Printing 10 9 8 7 6 5 4 3 2 1
Printed in Canada by Houghton Boston

DEDICATION

To Margaret Tracy Sinclair, named for her grandmothers.

ACKNOWLEDGEMENTS

It is impossible to list all the women I would like to acknowledge here. But in one way or another – through their conversation or their example – this book has been especially informed by the wisdom of the following remarkable women: Christel Markiewicz, Trisha Mills, Jane Howe, Elizabeth Frazer, Adelaide Saeger, Rose Tekel, Sarah Tector, Wanda Wallace, Kathy Aylett, Suzanne Brooks, Muriel Duncan, Diana Goodwin, Kimberley Robinson, Rhea Knapp, Carolyn Sinclair, Dorothy Tuttle, Norma Kozma, Sister Margaret Smith.

I owe Jim Sinclair a debt of gratitude for his patience, encouragement, and excellent housekeeping while this book was being written. In fact, I am grateful to all four Sinclair men – Jim, David, Andy, and Eli – who, along with Tracy, light up my life.

St. Andrew's United Church continues to be both my inspiration and my spiritual discipline. I am amazed at my good fortune in being part of this wonderful community.

GreenSpace North Bay, Friends of Sweetman's Garden, and the North Bay Civic League are made up of people of high commitment and laughter. I treasure the members of these organizations.

My friendship with the Podolsky family, with whom Jim and I share delight in young Eli, is a source of great pleasure.

I am grateful to Gulliver's Books and Toys for many fine book launches.

And as always, Wood Lake Publishing has been an inspiring publisher. I am very grateful to Ellen Turnbull, my patient and highly skilled editor, and gifted designer Verena Velten; I thank sincerely as well the others behind the scenes who join them to make Wood Lake Publishing a creative spiritual home for many, many readers.

INTRODUCTION

These daily mediations are for elder women, although I will be pleased if younger women listen in. They might want to know if there is a life as an elder woman.

I had to experience life as an elder for a few years before I could answer that question.

I am pleased to report that there is life, and plenty of it. While elder women still face many of the issues they experienced as middle-aged women, they have more freedom to consider them. I am still working, for example, to understand the emotional legacy of my parents, especially my mother. My elder years give me time to do that.

I have also come to realize the importance of elder women. One major job is to remember the past. The world has changed remarkably in the last decade. Social networking means that everyone can be in touch every minute. Vast amounts of data and the latest news are available at the click of a mouse. This is both convenient and world-altering. It means that, as individuals or nations, we find ourselves faced with rapid change and with having to make quick, hard decisions. Elder women can help because we have a long, and often practical, view.

Another important task is speaking out. We remember, for example, how after a terrible world war Canada developed the compassionate social system which is now in danger. Elder women can complain loudly when something mean and hard is stepping through the political life of the most tolerant country on earth.

Our memories of that open-hearted nation, of clean public water, of a sea filled with life, are crucial. How will our descendants re-invent for their own time the vision we knew first-hand unless we describe it?

In order to accomplish these tasks of our old age, women need to strengthen their own inner life. Our knowledge of climate change and damaged landscapes can lead to despair. It is our work as elder women to seek hope and offer it generously.

I find abundant hope in children and spouse and friends, in the wit and meaning of dreams. I see it in the resolve of young people who delight in caring for Creation. Hope abides in the arduous and tender love between mother and daughter and granddaughter, in the hard and necessary work of envisioning a community full of beauty, and in the joyful struggle to see God when our understanding of the spiritual is as slippery and temporary as ice.

This book is about all these things.

JANUARY 1 ❧ BEING AN ELDER

Being an elder is not about superior knowledge. As a journalist, I have learned a little something about an enormous number of topics, and a lot about a very few. To this day, I can blast a crater-sized hole through any dinner party, leaving all around the table dazed by the implications of global warming or Indian residential schools.

This does little good.

Wisdom is required, not information. Wisdom knows how to contain passion, much as the core in a nuclear reactor is contained by water. Wisdom is ancient, intuitive, and principled. It does not do harm. While it does not in itself do good, its application leads to good. It never bullies or intimidates, is never smug or arrogant. Wisdom is not damaged by failure or loss, although it may at times be hard to find.

Wisdom makes use of knowledge, but seldom allows it to show.

JANUARY 2 ❧ WINTER PRAYER

Thank you for winter, God. Even the hard parts: the bulky clothes to wrestle onto little children, the climb from the car over a snowbank to fumble a loonie into the parking meter, the ice. Without all this, there would be no sense of myself as a strong winter person.

Thank you for winters of the heart, when I wrestle with your seeming absence. Without this there would be no mornings when I leap out of bed surprised by my own strength and happiness.

I am grateful when you lead me to be your partner in your peaceable Kingdom, grateful for the chance to serve coffee, listen to a friend, and juggle the practicalities of bringing about the beautiful household of God.

I pray for the well-being of my neighbours. I pray that I may wrestle with your puzzling commandments: to love my neighbour and my enemy and myself.

I ask this in the name of Jesus. The one who walked on water loves my January lake. The one who smeared mud on a blind man's eyes loves my northern springtime. The one who loves all those who try their imperfect best loves me. Amen.

JANUARY 3 ❧ WASTING TIME

Now that I no longer have to struggle for a paycheque, I keep telling myself it is all right to attempt to write a mystery novel and perhaps – even likely – fail. Yes, I know it might be a waste of time. But it is okay to "waste" time now, if I want to.

Failing, though. That is awfully hard to do. This must be the hardest lesson of my seventh decade: how to fail gloriously, hugely, when every cell in my body yearns for a dignified and respected old age.

Real elders don't mind failure.

JANUARY 4 ❧ ELDER VOICE

Becoming an elder has nothing to do with wanting to be one, or seeking the role. You can't run for eldership. Elders arise out of the community by unconscious consensus.

And I think it is not the whole community that does this. It is merely a sizeable portion of a certain segment: the environmental group, or the churchgoers, the political junkies or the poetry readers. Some of these groups are smaller than others. I am not the most knowledgeable, nor even the most committed in any of these areas. I am passionate though; and most of the time, I listen. Preferably before I pronounce.

Some elders are extroverted and speak out easily. Some are introverted and don't.

In the end, to be an elder is to say what needs saying, whether or not it is comfortable to do so.

JANUARY 5 ❧ GRANDPARENTS

Every grandparent I know is addicted to his or her grandchildren. That includes me.

Perhaps this is our second chance at being influential with little children. This time we will get it right and nothing will interfere with all the good stuff – the cookie-making, painting, walking, or storytelling. Or maybe it is simply a joyous effort to help their parents when they don't have enough hours in a day to give everyone what they need.

And grandchildren make us feel young. (Look, I can still walk a stroller, slide down a hill, throw a child up into the air.)

They connect us with the future. Once they are safely here we can die, because we know we will continue.

JANUARY 6 ❧ EPIPHANY

This is the day the wise men reached Bethlehem. Their gift-laden arrival into the presence of the Holy Family is the conclusion of the nativity story, which itself is the first chapter of a life that would end with a heartfelt cry from Jesus to his Abba.

When our little grandson Eli was living in Jerusalem he learned the words Eema and Abba, which he called his Mama and Dada at least some of the time. His father said he used them when he was tired. Clearly these were words he had learned at daycare; but they became the default terms.

But now I know for sure that Abba really does mean Daddy.

JANUARY 7 ❧ MOTHER

This is the day my mother died. She was 96, a strong, talented woman who cherished her children and adored her grandchildren and great-grandchildren. She was also often irritable in her latter years, sparking similar irritation in me that I did my best to conceal.

Now I have work to do. I need to figure out why we were the way we were. I need to make peace with her. In my late sixties, I should be well beyond blaming her for any part of the way I am. But I do.

As a toddler, my mother had travelled with my grandmother from Vancouver to Northern Ontario. At age nine, she saw the great fire of 1922 devouring houses one by one down their street, stopped by a wind shift before it reached them.

After she married, she and my father lived in a small log cabin with a wood stove. My mother deeply missed electricity and indoor plumbing. She once threw a naphtha-gas-powered iron through the window, convinced of an imminent explosion.

They soon moved to a more comfortable setting where they lovingly raised my brother and me. When my father died, my mother moved close to me. She was welcomed at our friends' homes as a treasured elder for the next 23 years.

She grew more difficult with me. Perhaps I was one with whom she was able to be cranky, one she trusted would not desert her. Perhaps it was advancing blindness, discomfort, or her inner issues at work. I struggled to remember when this wasn't so. Now my work is to understand. This is my chance to learn her strength and love and – as much as I can – avoid passing on her pain.

JANUARY 8 ✤ CHILDREN

I remember this. My children were the saving grace between my mother and me. They visited her, teased her, loved her, were serenely (for the most part) aware of the pain I felt over the crankiness she and I seemed to create in each other. They remembered the young grandma who listened to their every word when they were little, and cheered them on in everything they did.

This was respite care for me. It was a miracle.

I would like to avoid my mother's desire to perfect her children – especially me, her daughter – long after the point where it might have been (vaguely) understandable. Surely we can give up perfecting our children once they are teens and able to think in an adult way. Surely we should never try to perfect our children.

Perfection is a vastly overrated state of being.

JANUARY 9 ✤ ELDER SENATORS

In Canada, senators could be elders. I suspect some of them are. One of the deep disagreements that I have with today's Conservative Party is its yearning to elect our senators, forcing a race for votes instead of an honouring of their accomplishments and experience-honed wisdom. It's an odd Darwinian streak in a party that has allies who doubt the theory of evolution. Democracy is admirable and essential. And there is a role in democracy for the simple appointment of those who have developed wisdom over the years but have little capacity to mount an election campaign.

If you don't believe in wisdom – just in aggression and brittle cleverness and individualism – then you won't believe in elders.

JANUARY 10 ❧ NEWLY NANA

I am happy," almost three-year-old Eli announced one day at breakfast. This made all of us happy. Then he sang, "It's a wonderful day for bones," his own composition. (He had been read to about bones and muscles and other bodily attributes.)

Life is an endless wonder. Eli has investigated every drawer and cupboard, except the ones up high where we keep truly dangerous stuff. I put it all away and he re-discovers it and drags it out again, to inspect, take apart, reassemble (not always possible), and thus leave a thin layer of detritus over every flat surface.

Mostly I am okay with this, although occasionally Neat Nana takes over and throws out the destroyed bits. It's difficult to get the balance back, after so many childless years, between generous access to intricate things – very important for small brains and fingers – and chaos.

JANUARY 11 ❧ AFTER SABBATICAL

It is necessary to discover a new structure to my days. I need to lift up my identity as a writer again, after putting it down for months. It was fun painting the house, room by room, after all those years of slitting my eyes closed so as not to see how badly it needed doing.

But I have felt restless since my grandson went home. I am not occupied with small hands helping me pat out cookies or roll out dough, or a small voice shouting, "AIG," so I won't forget to add the essential ingredients to the pancakes in the morning.

I miss it.

However, I am after all a woman of many parts. Not just Nana (although it is compelling at this time), not just Mamma (although I love that dearly), and not just Wife (although that is fun too, Baba and Nana together pushing Eli in his stroller in below-zero temperatures to get him to sleep).

As an elder, there is time to rediscover all that women are.

JANUARY 12 ❧ BEARS

There is no light until I pull the curtains
Hung to banish streetlight glow on snow.

In my cave, I sleep in darkness
Bear-like
Metabolism paused.

Morning is spring always.
I pull the curtains,

Grey plain dawn pours in.
My heart begins to tick again
Blood moves
Orange streetlight gone until tonight.

Mother bear pads around her den.

JANUARY 13 ❧ ELDER MENTOR

My elder for the last 30 years has been Christel Markiewicz. She fled to Canada from Germany after World War II, and has the hard-won wisdom of the survivor and self-taught scholar. We interpret each other's dreams and she expertly charts my stars, offering advice and the world's best apple cake.

The thought that I might be an elder myself never occurred to me until a local parents' group, trying to prevent the closure of a long-established neighbourhood school, wondered if the Sinclairs would address the school board. It is a fine school, within a short walk for most students, with a committed parents' group. So, "as elders who have seen the vital role this school plays," we talked about the value of walkable neighbourhoods.

It was the first time I had given myself that title. Elder. Was I being arrogant? I wondered. One friend listened patiently to my ruminations. "You're retired," she said finally. "Nobody can fire you. You can say what you want."

Christel believes that saying what you want is the elder's job. "We have to speak out when needed," she says, "whether it is politically correct or not." Otherwise, "we are missing our responsibility."

So she plumbs the stars and offers advice to individuals on anything from controlling impulsivity to avoiding dangerous falls. Lacking her arcane data, I say what I want about Creation in general. I am discovering that people with relatively little time left on this planet are acutely aware of its beauty. We are offended at the destruction of a forest in order to build something ugly. We make speeches about neighbourhood schools and tree cover out of the responsibility that Christel describes.

We are not cantankerous. We are just repeating what our years declare to be important.

JANUARY 14 ❧ WRITING TIP

Elders need to speak out well, so people will listen. That means we need to write as well as we can. In fact, I don't seem to have access to any wisdom I might possess until I do write it out. I look in surprise at the page thinking, "Hm. I didn't know I knew that."

My advice is to read well. Especially just before you have to write. It doesn't have to be on the subject you are about to embark on. (In fact, it's better if it is not, because you don't want to be echoing someone else's analysis.) Seek out clear, lucid, even lyrical writing that will settle into your head and become normal. You want to echo pure and beautiful communication so that people will be eager to hear what you say.

This may be especially important if – like me – you have a habit of omnivorous reading. I am a kind of deep dredger of the literary world, gulping down even mediocre prose for the sake of a fast-moving plot. If I am to avoid spewing all this back out when I want to inform an audience, I take care to swallow a bit of Sharon Butala or Annie Dillard before I sit down to write.

JANUARY 15 ❧ ELDER ECOLOGY

Our elder memories are especially valuable as the slow train of climate change chugs closer. Despite the difference in our ages, my 92-year-old elder Christel and I have experience in common. The sight of mud-encrusted rubber boots by the back door, for instance, packs a similar physical punch for us both. "I lived on the land and loved the land," she says. Fleeing war-torn Europe, she ended up near Timmins, Ontario, married to a dairy farmer. She wore her boots in the barn and the garden, where she grew "wonderful cabbage. And beets for borscht, and beans. Although sometimes the beans would freeze."

But the land we both love is changing. The climate is uglier, oil supplies are shrinking. A community's resilience in the face of such uncertainty may depend on knowledge that the elderly retain. Christel and I know how to grow vegetables, for instance, for the day when fuel for refrigerated trucks carrying supplies from Florida becomes too expensive.

We remember when just about everybody had a vegetable garden, and local farms were smaller and more numerous. We also know, in her words, "how physical work makes us happy. To sit on the hay load, bringing in the last one, the dog beside you, it's a good tired. You feel wonderful. There is something in it that you cannot buy."

JANUARY 16 ❧ A PLANET IN PAIN

This is what I believe. We live in a holy earth, created with just the right amounts of oxygen and carbon, water and heat to grow the food we need. Just as a baby thrives in its mother's womb, so we live in the womb of Mother Earth, utterly dependent on her for all our needs.

And she is in trouble. I recently picked up Bill McKibben's book *Eaarth: Making a Life on a Tough New Planet*. The earth as we knew it is gone, he says. The hydrological cycle in North America, for one example, has already changed so that in some areas we get terrible drought and in others devastating floods.

The womb we have lived in for all of human civilization has become less than friendly. We may, McKibben says, "with commitment and luck, yet be able to maintain a planet that will sustain some kind of civilization, but it won't be the same planet, and hence it can't be the same civilization."

We need, therefore, to tell stories. This is the way it was, we must say to our beloved young who cannot remember the sea abundant and the forests endless, dark, and rich. Our memory of Earth's nourishing womb must be retained so we can live in her again.

JANUARY 17 ❦ ELDER GIFTS

There will be no Rapture. Our salvation from climate change and famine does not involve some of us being whisked to a heavenly platform in the sky. I do not believe an angelic throng will arrive to rescue us, although I do believe in angels. It depends on us humans, us women, us faithful elders whose hearts are open to God's hope.

Elder women in this lovely, damaged world need to discern our gifts. We know many helpful things from our own beginnings in a smaller, local world – alike, in some ways, to the one that is arriving.

I remember my mother and father hanging out the laundry, pegging it to the line and letting sun and wind do the work of electricity. I remember Bible stories. We knew they were not history, but we also knew they held truths. The weak and small, these ancient texts declared, can defeat the Goliaths of this world. The weary and lost can be brought back to life, like Lazarus. The hungry can be fed.

These are stories for when giant corporations seem too strong and our leaders too bewildered.

Elders have the long perspective that brings hope.

JANUARY 18 ❧ SISTERHOOD AND CLIMATE CHANGE

I hardly ever pass along the inspirational sayings that arrive by email inbox from my dear women friends. I am, after all, in the business myself. I will write and send my own, or none at all.

But I love that they send them, that I am included on this or that sisterhood list. Women's ability to regard other women as sisters – even women they don't know – is now crucial. Some of our sisters are going to be in terrible straits as a result of climate change. The mosquito that carries dengue fever (an especially nasty killer of vulnerable people), for instance, now has a much larger geographic range thanks to warming temperatures. It has gone beyond Bangladesh and other parts of Asia and is appearing in Mexico, El Salvador, Uruguay, and Brazil.

We will have to figure out how to be in solidarity with our sisters who are damaged by this. And they will have to teach us their strength and skills as we embark on a simpler life.

JANUARY 19 ❧ WORDS

Each Sunday at church I am surrounded by beautiful words: hymns that we sing with varying degrees of skill, enchanted to say such words out loud; the sermon, soaked in research and inspiration and, frequently, wit; and the choir singing the words of our own choirmaster with joy because they love him and God. There is no other place I can go where I am surrounded week after week with poetry, wisdom, and passion. Words.

I am a fool ever to miss these words by sleeping in or avoiding a cold walk on a winter day.

JANUARY 20 ❧ BEING GROWN-UP

I imagine that when people die they are still wondering when they will feel completely grown-up. What is the definition of grown-up? Detached? Wise? Brave? Oh, I know how quickly I can be tossed back into a morass of childish fear and confusion.

I love the biblical story of the twelve-year-old daughter of Jairus, so needed and loved by her father that after she dies, he persuades the miracle-working rabbi Jesus to resurrect her. "Give her something to eat," the rabbi orders when she opens her eyes. It's hard work coming back to life. The young girl would be hungry.

Similarly, elders need to feed the hungry child within us, our own young self reborn after the many deaths suffered over years of adulthood. We need to giggle and take days off and write poetry. A young girl's enthusiasm and laughter for its own sheer sake is now required, if not always welcome. It gives us hope.

Elder women are not elderly all the time. And childhood is never without strength.

JANUARY 21 ❧ CHINESE NEW YEAR

Ever since our grandson was born and his grandfather began to greet his colleagues with wondrous tales about him, our friend Wenh-In Ng sends Eli a small red envelope with lai see or "lucky money" in it. This is a way of wishing him a prosperous year.

Our grandson is Jewish. His father is Christian. I am Christian, and my grandmother was Scots, therefore I am also Celtic. Wenh-In is a Chinese Christian who came to Canada in the 1960s. Baba is Christian, and his great-grandmother was Irish, and so he is Celtic too. His ancestors were Roman Catholic and converted to Protestantism when they came to Canada.

Surely Wenh-In's lovely gesture is a sign that humans are finding ways to treasure their own spiritual identity, and each other's.

JANUARY 22 ❧ HOW TO BUY A HOUSE

Buying a house or condo is a huge undertaking. It is wise when contemplating such a step to be attuned to the intangible, as well as the concrete matters of pipes and electricity. You could call this intangible the angel of the house: the unseen collection of memories and yearnings and desires that accompany every structure. Like houses. Or institutions.

The angel of my house, I think, is rather happy. The house is old and solid. It has not one but two sun porches, where one can sleep like a cat on a bright winter day. The angel of this house ignores the busy street and contemplates the large garden with a massive maple, planted early on for shade. The angel says we don't need air conditioning – the tree will do – and suggests we compost table scraps. It advises us not to turn the heat up high in winter because the sunny porches or the fireplace will do fine. The angel is fond of the old-fashioned dining room, where we gather to talk and eat and have meetings or read the paper over coffee.

Check with the angel as well as the home inspector before you buy. If you all agree, it's a good purchase.

JANUARY 23 ❧ DREAMS OF TRAVEL

As an elder with the luxury of time, I try to honour dreams. I write them down and meditate on them. This does not always produce a meaning but it encourages more dreams. After a while, a dream vocabulary is built up. Witness the following interpretation.

I dreamed I was in a new job and had to take part in a marathon of some sort. I ended up riding a stationary bike. Quite uncomfortable, especially as some elderly man needed something on the wall where I was, and pressed against me so I couldn't pedal. I was losing time!

Then I was going back to the office for the party. I rode a real bike this time. It was pretty much downhill and two women friends came behind and walked more slowly.

Somehow, in the training or marathon or whatever it was, I had broken my nose. It was purple and mostly covered with a huge plaster. Very broad, as if it had been squashed almost flat.

Travel dreams often point out a problem in the way the dreamer is getting through life. This one came when our family (like every family at some point) was dealing with a sudden crisis that turned out to be ongoing. Hence the "new job" and the "marathon."

Looking back (hindsight is wonderful) I see the dream was trying to tell me that I needed to get away from the "elderly man" – a figure symbolizing rules and regulations and individual power – because this aspect of my character was holding me back. I needed community (the "party") instead of trying to deal with this myself. I especially needed my two women friends. That would make things easier ("cycling downhill").

Of course, my dream warned me, none too gently, that pride is injured whenever we admit our weaknesses. Sharing my crisis – even with my two best friends – was like, well, breaking my nose.

It was a useful dream. We made it through that rough spot, my friends and me, "flattened" pride and all. And we will again. The crises I face in the day bring messages from God at night.

JANUARY 24 ❧ ON TENDERNESS

My husband is a skilled storyteller. But he has always been vulnerable to tears when speaking in public. I have learned to sit quietly and breathe while he pauses, struggling with a story that he finds moving.

He has a tender heart. Such a heart is a vastly underrated asset in a competitive, even brutal, age. To be tender is to risk being wounded. But tenderness is also contagious. When we feel vulnerable warmth towards another creature it leaks out all over and infects everyone. We all have to sit and breathe and wait and risk our own hearts cracking open.

Tenderness is not fashionable. It is precious though.

JANUARY 25 ❧ REPENTANCE

Repentance means, literally, turning around, a complete about-face. This word has many applications. For instance: I disagree fervently with one of the councillors in our city on almost every subject, from traffic control to parks. I am sure that I am enlightened, and she is not.

Then, at a council meeting, I watched a woman make a singularly uneven presentation. Clearly still in need of psychiatric care, she struggled determinedly to register her viewpoint on her care at the hospital where she had been a patient. (Never mind that this subject was not in the purview of city council.) Councillors, visibly uneasy with her subject and manner, heard her out but had no questions for her. Except for my usual suspect, the elected member with whom I can find little common ground. Her question, offered quietly, was "Would you like a hug?"

Yes, the presenter certainly would. The councillor got up, walked to the podium, hugged her gently, and they walked out together slowly, the councillor's arm around the other woman's shoulders.

I still disagree with this councillor's position on almost everything. But I have repented of my assumption of enlightenment.

JANUARY 26 ❧ WRITING TIP

In one of our periodic house-emptying sessions (why leave this for the children to clean out?) I found journals. Every member of the family kept journals, filled with endless pages of ideas and thoughts. I was impressed.

Women need to write. Ideas are always swirling around and we capture them. For a time, these reflective moments are safe from drying out and blowing away in a desert of trendiness.

That's why I worry about Twitter. The thoughts appear so fast, and are replaced almost at once. How will they ferment and become solid and rich?

JANUARY 27 ❧ CROSS-CULTURAL LEARNING

In my old age I want practicalities. The First Nations idea of grandparenting is such a one. Often grandparents in the First Nations community take heavy responsibility for the raising of the child when the parents are at a hectic stage in their lives. They expect this, and do not complain, but rejoice.

I like this very much. I emulate it when I can.

A whole generation is cared for by these older people. And they do not focus simply on being a grandparent by blood. Once, at a large and very serious conference, I saw a teenaged boy go trembling to the microphone to tell the gathered politicians – First Nations and not – that it was time to pay attention to the needs of youth like him on reserves. His "grandmother" accompanied him, keeping her hand firmly on his shoulder the whole time. His elder's presence gave him the strength to say what needed to be said.

She was not his "real" grandparent. But she was his by right. This form of grandparenting does not involve greeting cards or special days. It is serious, and vital, and practical.

JANUARY 28 ❧ FRIENDSHIP

Need shifts back and forth. They need help. We need help. When I was young and foolish I thought I would always be the rescuer, a role that I like very much. The strong one. Now – after a string of my own humbling crises – I rejoice in my friends' utter lack of schadenfreude, in their clear and voiced memory of the times they needed help, in their generous listening, listening, listening.

Now I understand that the strong are those who know when they need the attentive ear, the friends who can sink deeply into your pain and at the same time maintain their own anchored soul, in order to pull you back.

JANUARY 29 ❧ MATURITY

In Hebrew, *tsimtsum* means contraction of divine energy. Psychologist Wendy Mogel, in *The Blessing of a Skinned Knee*, writes that "originally, everything was God. God filled up the entire universe. But in order for one thing to exist, something else has to withdraw…So in order to make a place for the world, God had to withdraw a bit."

At first, Mogel explains, God stayed close to us, his new and vulnerable creations, to provide help as needed. When we were trapped by the Egyptians, God provided plagues; when we needed to escape quickly, God parted the Red Sea. God was a day-by-day, sometimes minute-by-minute miracle maker. Later, as we matured, God withdrew further and made fewer miracles. This was a good thing. This allowed humankind to grow up and understand that we must, however imperfectly, deal with the problems that confront us.

I believe we, and our political leaders, should act like grown-ups. We need to fully understand that no miracles will be forthcoming to save us from ourselves. Carbon dioxide concentrations in the atmosphere will not suddenly, miraculously, fall from 387 parts per million to something below 350 parts per million. Affordable housing will not suddenly appear in our municipalities. The cod will not suddenly reappear, nor the salmon.

God is still with us. But God expects us to be adults.

JANUARY 30 ❧ MATURITY (TWO)

What does a grown-up people look like? We plan ahead, not waiting decades to begin climate-change abatement or an end to child poverty. We discuss problems courteously, not shouting each other down. We co-operate, not insisting (for instance) that nobody can work on climate change until everybody is at the same developmental level. And we do not wait for miracles. We understand that there has been a divine contraction; God has pulled back so that we can have the room to get to work ourselves.

Perhaps maturity as a citizen is about accepting oneself and one's country as we really are, loving both unconditionally as we try each day to mend the world.

JANUARY 31 ❧ LOVE'S UNEXPECTED SHAPE

My daily newspaper has a section consisting of the well-edited story of a loved one's life, appearing weeks or months after their death. The passage of time must cool grief a little, because what shines out from these columns is not so much loss as continued blessing. They are a pleasure to read.

If someone writes one of these for me one day, I wonder how it will look. Will I be able to hold my own in this company? Will I have had sufficient grandchildren or even great-grandchildren, or accomplished enough in the relational realm, the world where what counts is not the number of books written or the speeches given, but the world in which we are loved?

But of course, there is no "enough" to live up to in this world of affection. The threshold of elderhood – the moment that you know you are one – is when you observe that you are simply rejoicing in who you are and who you love. Love, you realize in that instant, is not contrived by striving. It is not accomplishment. It just is.

Some of us will never marry. Some of us will never be parents or grandparents. Some of us who marry will meet divorce. Some will carry on and wish at times they hadn't. Most of us – perhaps all – will be surprised by the unexpected shape our family takes.

We need not be fooled by the culture into demanding that our lives take a certain course, and that all else is second-best. In the world of love and family there is no second-best, no sweepstakes to be won, no race that goes to the swiftest.

Elders know that. If they are wise, they will follow the First Nations example of treating all the young as grandchildren and then enjoy the response that follows. They will treat their friends with love, and discover they are precious family. And when they observe the unexpected shape of the love that surrounds them, they will say to themselves, happily, "It is fine."

Because it is.

FEBRUARY 1 ❧ IF I DIE TODAY...

Dying is something an elder thinks about. Suppose the angel was meant to come for me tonight, at midnight. (Raphael, I hope, the gentle guardian of those on pilgrimage towards God.) Not to complain – I have been granted sixty-eight years of days already, and in good health.

But how would I spend this day?

I think I would make pancakes for breakfast. Yes, pancakes, redolent with memories of canoe trips, and besides, Elijah loves them. Our little grandson, visiting, who awakens the rest of the household by whispering in their ears, "Pancakes. Cawfee (he pronounces it like his Brooklyn-raised other grandma). Bananas!"

Yes, on my last day, pancakes for breakfast, and my unsuspecting family home to visit for some holiday or other, all dawdling around the table, talking. We would solve the problems of the country over cawfee.

I hope someone writes the answers down.

And I would slip away to write a short last note to each. "Good-bye, I love you," I would say.

No surprise. They know that.

FEBRUARY 2 ❧ OR I MIGHT DIE NEXT SEASON

If I had one day left to live, what I would do would depend very much upon the season. My father, for instance, died in November. He dug the parsnips, put away his shovel, and closed the garden shed for winter. He took the train south to celebrate his grandson's birthday, came home, and died. I could do that. If autumn held my last day, I would do the same, sighing with satisfaction at our readiness for spring.

But perhaps it would be winter. Then I would go down to the lake a few short blocks away. Baba would accompany me, pulling Eli in the sled. I would ruminate in silent pleasure on my years with Baba-formerly-known-as-Jim. We would slide down the bank to the snowy beach and walk out on the ice, showing Eli how to walk on water.

For lunch we would have lentil soup and bread and hummus, which Eli loves. In winter I make soup and bread. The oven warms the kitchen, and the soup is cooled by putting it out the back door. I would put this advice in my notes to my family. But they know all that already.

Of course, it might be summer. If that were so, I would weed and deadhead, and dig some yellow iris for my neighbour who admires them. I would persuade Baba to mow the small lawn I have refrained from turning into perennial beds. He will appreciate it when they gather for the post-funeral party.

I will put that in my notes. Party party party. She died content. Rejoice.

But then again, it might be spring. Robins would sing all day. At midnight Raphael would come (sailing "between worlds and worlds, with steddie wing," as the poet Milton says) to carry me to God. We would talk. "But God is here already," I would say, pointing out the songbirds silent in the night.

And I would invoke the resurrection and refuse to go.

FEBRUARY 3 ❧ LATER

I did not see the holiness in my mother's dying until a year later. Many things are understood only after the passage of time.

FEBRUARY 4 ❧ MY MOTHER'S CHINA

My brother and I bought it for my mother, one piece at a time, when we were little. Someone – probably my dad – must have given us the money. Birthdays and Mother's Days and Christmas all meant a thin, translucent plate or cup and saucer, each picturing a tree in a stylized English garden setting.

This set belongs now to my daughter, but she is not ready for it.

Meantime, it sits in my dining room, a mute recollection of long-ago extended-family dinners. The small plates held apple pie and ice cream or – after I learned to bake – chocolate cake, at which I excelled. The large plates were laden with crisply cooked vegetables, grown in my father's garden, and elegant thin pieces of roast, carved with my father's sharp knife. My grandmother and assorted aunts and uncles would be there in a haze of cigarette smoke that slowly cleared as, year by year, they gave up smoking.

When we discovered that my brother was going blind, the plate at his place was illuminated with the brightest lamp in the house so he could see. Later, the light was turned to illuminate my mother's plate too.

Life went on. Laughter returned. The vegetables continued to make their way from the garden to the plate, crisp and bright. The roasts became more tender as money grew less tight. My father died, my mother died. The dishes remain.

When my children come home to visit, I will use these dishes.

FEBRUARY 5 ❧ RECOVERING

Recovery, says one veteran of a broken relationship, is a matter of taking it one half-hour at a time. Forget "one day at a time." It is half-hour by half-hour, just making it through, until strength reappears.

We are burned into wisdom by failure and loss.

No one in their right mind would wish for this. But if it is given, elders might as well enjoy the harsh wisdom we are granted.

FEBRUARY 6 ❧ RESPECT

Doctrine and dogma get a lot of bad press these days. Rightfully so, I guess. It's good to be wary of rules that make us rigid and unyielding. But sometimes I need a little straight-ahead standardized teaching about who God is and what God wants, even if I love the stories more. Even if I am constantly revising my notion about who and what God is. A group of my immediate elders in the faith wrote these words that I listen carefully to:

> We are called to be the Church:
>> to celebrate God's presence,
>> to live with respect in Creation,
>> to love and serve others,
>> to seek justice and resist evil...[1]

That third line was influenced by our First Nations elders. They know about respect. It reverberates for them, and I try to let it move through my bones too.

So even when I am angry with political leaders, I struggle to speak with respect. And I try to live with respect in God's created world. Even if my understanding of God shifts each day, it pleases me to place the world created out of love alongside the one resulting from colliding atoms.

Oh, I am not successful at respect. I rail at politicians and I forget to take out the compost and – rushing – I use the dryer on a sunny day. I drive to the store instead of walking, and when it's cold I allow the car to idle. I do a thousand other things that hurt Creation.

Without that rule *live with respect in Creation*, I would be worse.

FEBRUARY 7 ❧ RETROSPECTIVE WORRY

It's hard to be worker and mother. As an elder, I sympathize profoundly. Did my being a writer and spending so much of my time in a far place hurt my children, I wonder?

Probably. I try to be better now. I know I can't go back. I can mourn my mistakes and try to fix what I can, and go on. Go on. Guilt is not a productive emotion.

FEBRUARY 8 ❧ COLD

I love cold. I am not sure the other members of my family feel the same way. But loving the cold is an asset in northern Ontario, especially in a house whose previous owners, in the days of cheap energy, took "live better electrically" seriously.

Mostly all is well. Our 100-year-old house is well-insulated (for its time) and when the sun shines our south-facing windows capture plenty of solar heat. Still, on very cold, grey, windy February days, we put on sweaters. And long underwear and warm fleeces, and I find excuses to cook something, anything, in the oven, so as to have a reason to turn it on. We light a fire in the fireplace. This can't really heat the whole house, but it produces one warm room if the living room doors are shut. Sometimes I wear my long, warm, fleece dressing gown all day over my clothes, which startles unexpected visitors.

And I love this. I love knowing winter is winter. I love the fire, the mild scent of smoke and the crackle, and getting out flannel sheets and piling comforters on the bed, and – above all – I love knowing that (as a woman of a certain age) if I wake up steaming I can fling off all the covers and lie blissful in the cold air.

I love passing on these tips from my own childhood:

Cold air will not kill you.

Cold air does not cause pneumonia. Germs do.

Warm clothes are cozy.

Winter is different from summer. And that's good.

We are strong northern people. Rejoice.

FEBRUARY 9 ❧ GRATITUDE

Think gratefully about what almost, but didn't, happen. The time you realized you were speeding in a residential neighbourhood and slowed down before you hit a child. Be grateful. The last time someone you love had a cold and it didn't turn into bronchitis. Be grateful.

There. Sometimes we need to take a break from our arduous active worrying – which of course is what keeps our world safe – and be grateful for what we have accomplished with it.

FEBRUARY 10 ❧ POLITICS TIP

When attempting to mend the world – and we all should try to mend the world, even though we can never accomplish it – partner with other people and community groups who also have this in mind. Don't try to do it all yourself. This can make it fun, as opposed to terribly serious. Serious is an easy trap for social justice types.

Community activists have excellent potluck suppers. Children love them. Our middle son – many years away from home – encountered a potluck and said, visibly touched, "Ah! The food of my people!"

Writer Gwynne Dyer (*Future: Tense*) makes a case for cooperation on an international level. He says that along with environmental problems and climate change will come food shortages and refugee movements, even in "technologically competent parts of the world...so there had better be a system in place that enables us to spread the burden of coping with these changes." He was referring to the United Nations. But we can start creating our own systems to deal with local problems, aided by social networks whose happiest function is bringing real people face-to-face for homemade chili.

FEBRUARY 11 ❧ THE PLEASURE OF ELDERSHIP

Please. I don't want to read any more cute poems about failing memory and aching joints. Yes, that's part of getting older. But get over it.

The pleasures of eldership far outweigh the pains. Witness a recent meeting I attended. (Elders have more time to go to meetings, and the freedom to pick the interesting ones.) This was a meeting of activists fighting to save the urban forest. Each one loves this city. As we talked I felt constant little *zings* signalling delighted recognition of some fresh truth, some new facet of this or that person's passion for the earth. I saw a powerful oneness of purpose, even though some of us are young and some old.

We respect and enjoy each other. I know that elders have only a brief time to rest on our laurels, when people can still remember what we did (wasn't she a journalist or something?). Perhaps as that memory fades we will be relegated to that netherworld of unfunny poems about aching joints.

But not yet.

FEBRUARY 12 ❧ CHANGE

I have a photo of my mother as a telephone operator in the 1930s. She wore a long skirt and headphones. No callers could be connected without her voice and direct intervention.

I have no photo, but remember well the television set my science teacher built in the 1950s. It was the first I had ever seen. The screen was slightly tilted, which made it no less fascinating to me when I babysat his children.

We live a long way from those days. Technological change is getting faster all the time. Many elders don't bother to keep up. And why should we, I mutter to myself. Texting at the dinner table seems rude, and we've all endured the discomfort of the cell phone user in the airport lounge shouting his or her business at full volume.

What's an elder to do?

I consider my mother. Unable to see, she acquired a DAISY reader on which to play MP3 versions of the novels and histories she enjoyed. Although she frequently knocked it off the table trying to pound it into submission, both she and the machine survived the steep learning curve as she learned to use it.

She kept up, fiercely, when the technology was useful to her. I will do the same.

FEBRUARY 13 ❧ BEST IS LAST

It is interesting how the best insights often come at the end of an evening's conversation, when everyone is tired. Perhaps our desire to say something fresh and previously undiscussed in tandem with the loosening of safeguards that we associate with wine and sleepiness allow us to go a little deeper inside ourselves to see what is there.

Elders might have an edge here. We have accumulated a fine collection of bits and pieces of wisdom. Also, we are more tired.

FEBRUARY 14 ❧ MARRIAGE ADVICE

Elder women spend a remarkable amount of time around weddings and engagement parties. We have seen many Valentine's Days. We mutter to each other about who is seeing whom, and we keep caught up on the romantic entanglements of our own generation (don't think for a moment that it ever ends) and the ones that follow. From all this, I have gleaned some advice about marriage.

Marry someone you like.

Marry someone who enjoys some of the things you enjoy. Children, for example, or whales. Dreams, or rocket ships, airplanes, or hiking, or canoeing, or politics.

Marry someone who surprises you, if possible. Surprise and laughter are related and you will certainly need the latter.

Marry someone you respect. It's hard to forge respect later, when the flaws that are hidden beneath the sheen of early love begin to surface.

Marry a good cook. Or a good carpenter, or a good painter, or furniture refinisher, or gardener, or something. Someone who can hang a door or bake bread – who loves beauty and working with their hands (even if the rest of the time they lecture to students or sell stocks) – has redeeming features.

I could be wrong. But if you offer these rules at your next coffee hour, you won't run out of conversation.

FEBRUARY 15 ❧ HOLY LAND

When Elijah was here
This was the holy land.
The plane fled like an angel to Jerusalem
Bearing him.

Now there is – only recently – the holy land.

And here with its granite and birch and waiting snow
Here is yet holy,
Golden birch leaves slopping on the ground.
Here is the city of God

waiting the return of the small One.

FEBRUARY 16 ❧ FEAR

Since my mother died, I have been looking back, trying to understand why we were sometimes so irritable with each other. What were we thinking?

I suspect – for my part – I was reacting out of fear. When I saw my mother, I saw myself in 30 years. A healthy elder has a good life, until it's not. Until the hearing goes, along with the ability to walk downtown. As my mother declined, her frail presence announced to me that I too would weaken and die one day.

I have no way to know what motivated her sometimes sharp ways, but I suspect it was – again – fear. She may have feared being forgotten. Perhaps we all fear that when we die no memory of us will linger. I will remember her, though. My memories are locked in the bits and pieces we did manage to cram into our house, her cedar chest and paintings and books. Most of all, the good times and laughter are locked into our hearts. We won't forget.

When I am very old I must remember this, though. The enemy is not death, but fear.

FEBRUARY 17 ❧ GRANDKID TIP: LISTENING

Once I spoke harshly to my grandson Eli. I don't do this often. But he was resisting going to bed, and I was tired.

The next morning he hopped into our bed, snuggled between us and said, "I am sad when we are not friends."

Bewildered, I mumbled something forgettable and sleepy.

But later, I had that sinking, missed-opportunity feeling. "I am sad too, when it feels as if we are not friends. But we are." Is that what I should have said? Or, "You feel sad, and so do I, when we are upset with each other." Or, "Sometimes friends argue, but they love each other and get better." Or, "I know, Eli, when we love each other and we don't get along, it feels awful."

Reflect his feelings. Assure him of my love. All my old parenting dicta raced through my head. I wanted so much to do better, because we have figured out – by the time we have grandkids – that children have long memories that they do not always accurately interpret. The lens of childhood is extremely keen and slightly distorted. Somehow, I needed to give him a finer lens, one transparent to the reality that sometimes Nanas don't bounce well, and small children need sleep.

With the help of our strength and experience and love, children can bear reality.

FEBRUARY 18 ❧ CELEBRATION

I love the fact that Jesus was a Jew, because celebration is a cornerstone of Jewish faith. We are called to delight and celebrate and party over the fact of God's wonderful Creation.

Christianity has often prized self-denial over joy. I am trying to unlearn this by reaching back to the roots of my faith. I am trying to learn to pause and breathe and look around and choose something each day to party about.

It's not hard. Today snow glints from every tree, there is no wind, the sun is warm, the snowbanks sculptured. It calls for a long walk, humming. My faith demands it.

FEBRUARY 19 ❧ SEED ORDERS

The seed catalogues have been arriving since before Christmas. No matter how busy I am, this month I am overwhelmed by the urgency of it all. Gather up the catalogues, contemplate the varieties, picture the summer garden. Order the seeds.

The Kingdom of God is at hand. My feverish vision of a front yard swarming with poppies is a work of the imagination. Peace and beauty and fruitfulness are nearby, just over in the next dimension. I know this. And that Kingdom cannot be realized unless I can imagine it.

Long ago now, in *The Educated Imagination*, literary critic Northrop Frye explained how, when the imagination flourishes, "the world we live in and the world we want to live in become two different worlds. One is around us, the other is a vision inside our minds, born and fostered by the imagination, yet real enough for us to try to make the world we see conform to its shape."

Frye's words assure me that I can dream an alternate universe into existence. My poppies will light up the street. My neighbours will stop to visit and wander through the garden. Skateboarding teenaged boys will mutter – out of the sides of their mouths as they pass – "nice garden." Because gardeners imagine what Frye calls the "real form of human society," where fossil fuels are doled out with exquisite care and my grandson solemnly picks tomatoes into a bowl, they imagine the Kingdom of God into being.

If you get a seed catalogue, treat it as holy text.

FEBRUARY 20 ❧ IN OLD AGE

A few years ago our grandson came to visit, so his auntie and uncle arrived from several provinces away, and his great-grandmother came from her retirement residence across town. There was conversation, laughter, the clinking of glass and china – until one of our offspring, turning from interviewing Grandma about *her* accommodation, asked where I plan to live in *my* old age.

I had given the matter some thought. Really.

"I'm going to build a nice garden shed," I allowed, "and which-ever of you needs a house can live here in this one...(pause for the punch line)...and I will live in the shed and appear from time to time for a hot meal."

Silence around the table. Apparently retirement living is no laughing matter.

In fact, my kids, and yours if you have them, can see a slow train coming, and it's full of folks with bad knees. American researcher Sharon Brooks says that at least one million of the coming Baby Boomers in her country will live to be a hundred, and "many will live to a 'natural cap' of 120 years plus."

No wonder my children aren't laughing. That's a long time of coping with Mom and Dad, especially if their aching bones make them cranky.

But I was serious about the garden shed. A nice one, I mean. The saving grace in this is that wise elders give up their yearnings to have it all, and we simplify. I can live in a small space as long as I can talk to trees.

FEBRUARY 21 ❧ DIFFERENTIATION

As my mother grew older we instituted a regular Sunday evening supper with her. She looked forward to it, and it reminded me that she needed the pleasure of anticipation as much as the actual expedition to our house.

Sometimes I invited my aunt as well. My mother didn't like this, so I usually deferred to her wishes and seldom included my aunt, even though she had no other family in the city. My mother wanted us all to herself, and that is understandable. I understand what it is to be possessive about one's family, from my own greedy heart.

But – looking back – I wish that I had stood up to my mother more firmly. It would have been helpful to me, in terms of learning to set clear boundaries (never one of my strong points). I could have practiced setting limits by explaining to my mother that the guest list was my concern.

It would have been helpful to offer these two elderly ladies (who inhabited the same apartment complex, although not the same unit) a neutral space to enjoy themselves. They tended to be prickly with one another on their own ground.

It might even have been valuable to have considered the family dynamic at work here, clearly rooted in the past. Since it is my family, that dynamic affects me as well. Without intervention, the embedded patterns and deep issues of one generation don't stop. They go on to affect all the generations that follow.

It would have been especially good if I had probed – gently – my mother's feelings. Was she feeling lonely and unloved but was unable to tell us? I could have reassured her of my love, instead of allowing a separation between me and my father's sister.

Even though my mother and my aunt have died, I can still learn. It's not too late, I tell myself. I can learn to be firm and clear and self-directed while lovingly connected to my family.

FEBRUARY 22 ❧ DECORATING

I like to move furniture around and climb ladders and arrange green plants and interesting plates found at garage sales.

This sometimes wars with my social conscience. "What are you doing THAT for?" it sneers. "You SHOULD be out marching in the streets."

True, injustice reigns in many corners.

But women need both bread and roses. We need to rise like bread dough that will be used to feed the people. And we also need to eat that bread in beauty, putting our strong backs into creating a piece of art in which to live.

Why march, if not for beauty at the end?

FEBRUARY 23 ❧ READING THE NEWS

I try to practice saying "REALLY?" when I watch the news or read the daily paper. I try to read widely and cultivate questions like, "Who benefits from this?" Above all, when an interviewee says, "To be perfectly honest...," I long ago learned to hear alarm bells.

Nothing is ever perfect, especially honesty.

FEBRUARY 24 ❧ HOME

My home is Northern Ontario. I was born here, and I have paddled its waterways and sunned like an old turtle on granite outcrops. I needed no comfort but a thin beach towel. The bones of my mother and father and my grandmothers and my grandfathers are all here.

I love the sharp, distinguished seasons of this country. Here, you know the date by the colour of leaves, the weight of heat, or bite of cold. You could never mistake November for March, even though both are marked by the absence of leaf cover. The light is different. The birdsong and the seeds and sprouts and damp and dawn are utterly distinct one season to another.

But my daughter lives in the rain forest. Snow is a temporary miracle. Ice, if it appears at all, is a treacherous skim over lakes, not the stuff of fishing shacks and long Sunday snowshoeing and skating.

As I grow older my heart is pulled towards her.

I wonder if one's home can change.

FEBRUARY 25 ❧ THE KING'S SPEECH

This is Oscar season. I love movies. When I recommend them to my children, they laugh, because I never met a movie I didn't like. If all else fails, I can describe its sociological importance.

So I saw *The King's Speech*, in which Colin Firth plays King George VI and Geoffrey Rush his talented speech therapist. It is quite in order for me to praise this movie here (although my children did laugh) because any reader will always be able to see it. It will be a television staple forever.

The thing is, the King stammered horribly. Being an elder, I can remember how my childhood classrooms always had a picture of George VI hanging at the front. Also, we sang *God Save the King* every morning. (Stop laughing.)

I didn't know about his stammering. I did hear his speeches – not the wartime ones, I was too young, but his later Christmas addresses. When I found out that he had been terrified to speak in front of crowds, I was overwhelmed with understanding. My own tendency, confronted with a crowd to whom I have to say something – anything – is to faint. Not always, just enough to make life interesting for those who know me well. (Will she or won't she?)

The King managed (breathing, pacing, inwardly swearing) to overcome his handicap enough to do his kingly job. I managed to do the same with my more humble occupations. I never thought to try swearing.

Now I have a sense of comradeship with a king. And that's one of the tasks of art, including film. "Only connect," says E.M. Forster to the aspiring novelist. Only see how we are all human beings together, rich and poor.

And sometimes it is fear that binds us to one another.

FEBRUARY 26 ❧ WRITING TIP

For many years women's wisdom based on women's experience wasn't worth much. We were encouraged in those days to seek out professors and learn true knowledge.

But the sheen is off formal book learning. Two clicks of a mouse and I can find out what I need to know about almost anything. What counts as much, now, is our ability to think for ourselves.

Elder women know how to do this. We can stop regurgitating old authorities and consider our dream lives and the insights that came to us while holding a small child. We can sift out what's valuable from our own grandparents' stories, and we can read the newspaper (online or on paper) with a jaundiced eye and a letter to the editor forming in our heads.

Oh, we should never neglect the professors, both women and men. Their academic knowledge is still true. Allied with our own, it can change the world.

FEBRUARY 27 ❧ LIGHT

The German mystics thought of God as light. I know why. I am by a window, overhung by the dark winter maple, huge branches piled with snow. More snow falls from a white sky. There is nothing but white and black and quiet and light. This light does not sparkle or call attention to itself – it is the opposite of a sunny day – but it permeates everything, and it is profoundly calm.

Feminist theologian Dorothee Soelle chose to think of God-as-light because light is neither male nor female. It is not violent or commanding. Not a King.

When my young grandson asked me what God looks like, I said God was the cloudy pillar who led the people out of Egypt. Another time, though, I will say God is the light on a snowy day, the peaceful quiet white that makes me think of Eli and our big chair by the window, the light for reading stories.

FEBRUARY 28 ❧ PEAK OIL

Here is a bleak thought to match a February day. We are running out of oil.

Peak oil is the term for that moment when the total global supply of oil is gushing forth as generously as possible. After that moment – some experts feel it has already passed, while others suggest it will occur around 2020 – the rate of production will decline, because all the accessible oil will be gone. Just about everyone agrees that "peak oil" refers to a reality. The earth's store of fossil fuel is finite, and we will have to learn to live as communities without it.

This is where elders might be helpful. Some of us may remember when most travel was by train and air travel was a really big deal. We may remember how to fertilize our gardens with manure, not chemicals. And we can survive a winter without fresh strawberries. Really.

If we stretch our memories hard, we know that there were summers without air conditioning – we just moved slowly when it was very hot – and our grandparents planted trees that cast their shade over the house.

I don't mean to make it sound easy. No shade trees are tall enough to shelter high condo towers or office buildings. I dislike bus travel, and I have not yet surrendered my car. But the great public enterprise – and elders understand public enterprise, collective action for the good of every citizen – of moving a great many people and goods by rail might have to be revived.

Maybe we will have electric cars, of course, and a source of cheap electricity to fuel them. But the oil is not going to last forever.

FEBRUARY 29 ❧ CURIOSITY

My mother didn't want to die. I believe one reason she wanted to live was that she was so involved with the larger world that she simply wanted to live in it as long as she could. The fact that her involvement was limited to what she heard on the CBC or in her talking books made no difference. We would go to visit her and she would describe with absolute fascination things she would never see.

Once we were on our way to British Columbia and she insisted that we watch out for the white bears. We humoured her, knowing full well there was no such creature. Until we got there and heard about the ghost bears of the temperate rain forest, the recipients of a recessive gene that meant about one in ten was white, even though all their brothers and sisters were black.

Sometimes my mother would forget to say hello when we arrived. (HELLO!! I would shout, attempting to change this behaviour. Whatever for, I wonder now.) She would just burst into animated discussion of her latest reading material. It is a clue to me about how to live eldership well, even at the end. Stay engaged.

MARCH 1 ❧ ELDER PSYCHOLOGY

There are so many of us who are over 65. And we have pensions. Nobody can fire us. So we have the immunity required to say what needs to be said. Also, we have more time to devote to generativity, the generous care for the young that is the mark of a healthy old age.

Many of the young in my community are concerned about our environment. They want parks and walkable neighbourhoods. They want their children to be able to swim in the lake, and they want wildlife corridors so that damage to animal habitat from new home construction is mitigated. As an elder it is my work to join them.

I have discovered – humbly – that such activism in one's own community is harder than I thought. A journalist can always feel accomplishment from a met deadline. A volunteer working close to home encounters endless partial victory or defeat.

I find it especially difficult to address anything threatening my own precious neighbourhood. It is so close to my heart that it's hard to speak through the tears. It is less embarrassing to try to protect legacies belonging to the entire city: a pristine lake, an historic public garden, or ancient portage. These I can love without crumbling when I describe their value.

MARCH 2 ❧ AN ELDER AT HOME

I suppose it is the household goddess in me, never far from the surface: I love the neatness of organizing my very life into categories. For instance, the fact that we fit into one personality type or another objectifies our conflicts with our loved ones. (I like to stay home and visit with one person at a time. My spouse likes parties. I am an introvert. He is an extrovert. It's not my fault! Or his!)

My favourite set of categories is developmental stages. Stages of grief, stages of religious development – all fascinating ways of organizing my otherwise messy existence.

So I admire the work of psychoanalyst Erik Erikson. He envisaged nine stages which we negotiate as we move through life. The task for an elder (at least the last challenge before the final stage of dying) is to achieve a state of generativity, in which care for the next generation is paramount. Failure to negotiate this stage results in a sense of stagnation.

Which explains the passion with which I offer to carry boxes if my children are moving, my interest in painting walls, baby-sitting, making meals, anything, including unrequested advice.

They view this effort at generativity with kindness. I try not to consider the day I can't do this anymore, the day my categories fly apart. Erikson labelled this last stage *Integrity versus Despair*. I will be looking back over a life with which I can feel satisfied, or not.

So I try to remember that my time is short. It is better to save a lake than try to perfect my children. They must negotiate their own life stages for themselves.

If only my tidy housewife self wouldn't get in the way.

MARCH 3 ❧ DREAMS OF WEAPONS

It's a good idea to be alert after a dream about guns. Not because you're likely to meet an assassin, but because they contain a clue about one's unknown side. This dream, for instance:

I dreamed I was in a clearing and had to talk a gunman out of his gun. For some reason I was not afraid, although I was worried that the people on whose behalf I was intervening would suddenly break ranks and shoot him after I had talked him down.

For years my dreams have pointed out my tendency to "shoot people down" in conversation. I am absolutely unaware of doing this in my conscious life. Only when a dream calls my attention to it later do I remember, to my chagrin.

In this dream I have made some progress. (I would hope so, after all these years.) My conscious self (the light-filled "clearing" in the dark forest of my unconscious) is trying to stop me from interrupting someone or weighing in with know-it-all statements.

But every dreamer is a complex system. We humans are composed of many parts. So even as I struggle to tame my destructive side, other aspects of my personality are getting ready to "break ranks" and shoot. The fact that this takes place "after I had talked" is only too indicative of where I have trouble.

MARCH 4 ❧ THE FAITH OF OUR ELDERS

Some elders you never meet in person, but they arrive when needed. Old-time mission work, and religion itself, was distinctly out of favour by the time I stumbled upon the vivid letters of Victoria Cheung, a missionary doctor to South China in 1923.

I fell in love with her, right there in the archives where I was doing research. In the excerpt here, Cheung – a second-generation Chinese Canadian – was one of the few Western missionaries remaining after the Japanese invasion. Times were hard.

Kongmoon, South China
May 7, 1940
Dear Miss Buck:

Thank you for your letter of March first, with drafts enclosed...the hospital needs every cent it can lay hands on. Prices are soaring sky-high; quality diving to third-rate and lower; and you're fortunate to be able to get things. Price of rice has jumped from $85.00 yesterday to $100.00 today. Money market has gone to pieces.

With kindest regards, I am

V Cheung.

Cheung is unaffectedly brave and good-humoured:

> ...Just received the long looked for letter of Miss C's. She says they can't get eggs in Macao, and she's having an intensive diet of bacon and bread for breakfast. Fortunately we have our own hens, but we haven't learned how to make your kind of bacon yet, though the sisters have treated us to home-made smoked pork, which was good. I've had ample opportunity of learning how to raise pigs, my office overlooks the private wards which are now harbouring our pigs. If worst comes to worst, I'm going to the country to raise pigs, but you will have to return my retirement fund for capital, and I'll invite you to a bacon and egg breakfast.

She survived the occupation, and China's 1949 revolution, in her storefront clinic. The final entry in her file was scribbled at the top of her last letter: *Victoria Cheung died of lung cancer in 1967.* But her letters remained. Her humour and courage and practicality and love were compelling aspects of the religious life.

I decided to not give up on religion. I needed to learn this elder's generative, loving qualities.

> ...The girls are interested in baking, they make good bread and pies and are anxious to try cakes and pies and want ME to coach them, same tall order as the evangelist gave me last week, 7 new hymns, one for each morning! We got through and that is how I happen to be free to write to you. ...One of the babies is showing her first tooth. [2]

MARCH 5 ❧ GETTING CRANKY

All illogical
My bad temper is like

a stone tossed into a calm lake
a squawking bird that flies through the scene, wrecking it

A weed in the pristine border.

A red flag
A yellow marker
A blaze on a tree
A horrid neon stop sign
An enormous ugly billboard advertising discontent.

Rain helps.
A raging wind can take out the billboards.
Go on then, get it over.

MARCH 6 ❧ HAPPINESS AND PRIVILEGE

Some nights I come home after a simple, ordinary meeting counting blessings. I miss my own daughter, a country-width away, and so it is a pleasure to see the young women at the meeting expressing themselves with the dignity and wisdom

I see in her. I remember a meeting in East Germany where the participants expressed themselves honestly, in the face of the inevitable Stasi presence. So I understand it is a blessing to meet like this without fear of reprisal.

Why are we not deliriously happy here? We can express ourselves without massing in the streets or getting shot.

MARCH 7 ❧ PURIM

When our grandson was very little we accompanied him and his parents to a Purim celebration in Jerusalem. Eli was dressed up in a toque and a plaid jacket with his beloved stuffed moose pinned to his shoulder. In a crowd of small people wearing Queen Esther or cowboy costumes (the former a reasonable Purim costume; the latter, not so much) he was immediately recognizable as a Canadian.

The *Megillah* was read, the long story of Queen Esther saving her people. The children, sitting on the floor in the middle of the large congregation, cheered at the name of Esther. They booed and rattled their *ra'ashan* (noisemakers) whenever the dreaded name of Haman (whose attempts to destroy the people are documented in the story) was spoken. At such an early age they are included in the work of stamping out evil. The story is embedded in their bones.

It's not so different, I thought, from the pageants in my church, in which the youngest baby plays the child in the manger, and the older children are angels and shepherds and sheep. At such an early age the story is embedded in their bones.

All this makes me believe that we are not done yet with religion. Stories strengthen our bones and hold us together.

MARCH 8 ❧ PERSISTENCE

The Parable of the Persistent Widow
Then Jesus told his disciples a parable to show them that they should always pray and not give up. He said: "In a certain town there was a judge who neither feared God nor cared what people thought. And there was a widow in that town who kept coming to him with the plea, 'Grant me justice against my adversary.'

"For some time he refused. But finally he said to himself, 'Even though I don't fear God or care what people think, yet because this widow keeps bothering me, I will see that she gets justice, so that she won't eventually come and attack me!'"

One of my elders is a thin woman named Lorraine, a widow whose frequent back pain in no way slows her down. She reminds me of the persistent widow in scripture. She is always ready to write or visit our Member of Parliament, advocating support for gay marriage or cheap AIDS drugs for Africa. She asks questions, soaks up political knowledge, and uses it. A call for help at city hall brings her out with her friends, filling seats and being a presence.

Her back hurts. Did I mention that? It does not deter her. I keep her in my heart for those days when my knees hurt, or my neck, and I want to give up and stay home.

Persistence, bothering, justice. They all go together.

MARCH 9 ✺ TIME IS SHORT

My sense of purpose, as an elder, is heightened and intensified by my knowledge that the time remaining in which to be useful is short. There is no way around this. We receive the wisdom of age hand in hand with the knowledge that life is short, and getting shorter.

I embarked with a like-minded group to travel an historic portage. The weather was a fine mix of sun and cloud. We saw a deer. Despite my increasing age I paddled and hiked and proudly carried a pack. Only one moment – kneeling with others for a simple photo – nearly killed me. My knees hate that now.

Elder-work includes the ability to pretend, as long as possible, that we can live as if nothing hurts.

MARCH 10 ✺ DINNER AROUND THE TABLE

Someone gave my daughter a lovely, round, old oak pedestal table. I am yearning to spend a week just sanding and refinishing it for her, as it is somewhat battered. Maybe next time I visit.

Friendship happens while sitting around a table small enough that you can reach out and touch others and easily hold hands for grace. Children can climb up and hug everyone.

The circle is very important. There is no hierarchy in a circle. Consider the medicine wheel, symbol of wholeness. And in dream work, the circle is a symbol of the divine.

If you dream of bicycles, or if someone gives you a round table, consider it a holy moment.

MARCH 11 ❧ GIVING ADVICE

It is absolute folly to think we know what is best for another human being. Suppose they take your advice and it turns out to be disastrous?

On the other hand, sometimes we are experts in the field. Then is it okay to risk it? What if the advice just turns them away from your solution? I know that I, for one, stubbornly ignore advice if I have not sought it. This has not prevented me from foolishly offering counsel to equally independent offspring, with predictable results.

My advice is to not give advice.

MARCH 12 ❧ MYSTICISM

As a young man of 21, my brother discovered that he was going blind. Irrevocably, slowly, the area of his eyes available to him for vision would narrow until there was nothing left. We were all devastated.

And then one day he was in church, in our little congregation in Northern Ontario, a member of the choir. There was a large wooden cross behind him. He became aware, he says, of the figure of the Christ coming down from the bare cross to hold him, saying, "You are mine, and I am with you." For my brother, it was for a few moments the sole reality of that Sunday morning. And then the vision was gone.

My brother is now 71 years old. He has been completely blind for a very long time. He is one of the most content and least despairing people I have ever met. He seems to carry within himself some gene of happiness which underpins his competence in many areas. He is a valued artist, sculptor, and craftsman, and has spent his life after retirement as a highly regarded volunteer – abetted by my sister-in-law. They enjoy one other.

Dorothee Soelle, the great German theologian, says that mystical experiences – direct encounters with God – are not extraordinary. She says that thousands of people in other cultures have had such experiences, experiences of happiness, wholeness, this sense of being at home in the world, of being at one with God. But, she says, we don't have the language or even opportunity to talk about these remarkable moments. We can't explain them, and we let them go. It was years after the fact that I heard that story from my brother.

This might be a good subject for quiet morning meditation: When did I last encounter God?

MARCH 13 ❧ GOING TO CHURCH

It's not very trendy. Going to church used to enhance one's reputation. Now a confession of church attendance sometimes attracts the pity formerly reserved for the tragically naïve. (Poor thing. She believes those old stories.)

Well, yes. Because here, as pirates used to say, be treasure. I know this when I hear a friend reading the day's scripture and I feel it ringing through my body like a bell.

...the leopard will lie down with the goat,
the calf and the lion and the yearling together;
and a little child shall lead them. (Isaiah 11:5, 6)

This is the vision I had almost lost. This is the poetry of sustainability that Transition Towns[3] and other green movements have been seeking. The kings of capitalism will live in solidarity with the poor, and humans

...will neither harm nor destroy
on all my holy mountain.

MARCH 14 ❧ THE GARDENER

Beauty escapes from her fingers
like auras from a ghost
and
memory leans from the vines that curl under her hand
and
Ah! The taste of grapes and beans, the scent of lilac.

Hands age and wrinkle and the knees freeze
but still the slight warm odour of decay heralds a new season and
my fingers unleash light.

MARCH 15 ❧ TOMORROW'S CHURCH

I arrived late at a planning meeting for a women's congregational retreat that I had agreed to lead. The group had already decided how it would be. They would begin with singing, they said, "at least three-quarters of an hour of it. Our lives are busy and we need it."

And I was to talk about prayer. And we would actually do that. Pray.

Fine, I said.

In the afternoon we would braid sweetgrass that was already being collected from fields nearby. We would also have a sweetgrass ceremony. Did I want to lead?

"No," I assured them hastily, fearing that, since I am not First Nations, this would be disrespectful. They agreed they would invite a guest who had been learning for a long time from one of her elders.

They requested an Easter story.

"You mean, about the tomb and the angels," I said.

"No, no," they replied, "not *that* Easter story. It's June. We mean a story about someone who undergoes a great crisis and rises again. And we'll close with a Taizé-type service."

This is the new church. These women were perfectly aware of their spiritual needs. They knew that they needed lots of singing, lots of the music of joy. They knew that the Christian story of dying and rising still plays out in the lives of women today. They knew they wanted to integrate the long-ignored spiritual traditions of this land into their worship. They would have candles and flowers and fabric and music and food and the scent of sweetgrass.

Church will have this freedom and wholeness if it is to live on.

MARCH 16 ❧ CRISIS MANAGEMENT

I am pretty good in a crisis, ask anyone who knows me. For a day. Then I fall apart. It's good to know your patterns, because we all have crises. No one escapes. So if you know how you are going to behave, you can manage your own anxiety at the worst times by muttering that, "this will be more manageable tomorrow."

It appears that I am first of all protected by a kind of trance – the zen of crises – that enables me to offer coffee, serve food, make soup, and sound chipper. Then I begin to worry and grieve. That's no fun, but it is necessary. It's good to have a friend who will sit with you then and not run away from your pain – which is harder than it looks because if they love you, your pain will afflict them as well.

But it's also good if you can confine this grieving, however you do it (talking? crying?), to a small group of friends. Otherwise a vast crowd of people will be treating you like glass, and it becomes hard to see your own strength.

It's all very delicate. If you hide the painful feelings too deep, including from yourself, they will get stronger and more dangerous and erupt when you aren't expecting them. If you wear them like ritual robes or a *chador*, people will forget what you look like. Balance, balance, and totter home as best you can.

MARCH 17 ❧ SAINT PATRICK'S DAY

I've always been a little suspicious of Saint Patrick. Getting rid of all the snakes in Ireland seems to upset the balance of nature. And now that we are a little more relaxed with pagan deities, his work of converting the Irish to Christianity in the fifth century doesn't seem so noble.

So it is a relief to discover that much of Patrick's biography may have been fictitious. Monks eager to concoct a back story for Ireland's Christianization made him a legendary hero. It seems his famous use of the shamrock as a method for explaining the nature of the Christian God may have been a myth. The shamrock was in fact a sacred plant for the earlier Celts, and symbolic of their triple-faced Goddess, Brigit, and her sisters.

Not that I am downplaying the power of myth, or wish to miss an excuse to celebrate. I always gave my Irish-descended mother-in-law a shamrock plant on March 17, and she always greeted this with grateful amusement. She was a wise woman, and no doubt understood that a day of marching bands and silly hats is beneficial.

As for me, I am happy to overlook Saint Patrick's conversion efforts and revere the shamrock as a holy arbiter of all the green and growing things that come to life this month.

MARCH 18 ❧ SAINT PATRICK REVISITED

I do admire Saint Patrick greatly for his "Deer's Cry," in which he joyously sings of the power of Christ to protect him:
Christ with me, Christ before me, Christ behind me,
Christ in me, Christ beneath me, Christ above me…
Legend has it Saint Patrick was on his way to Tara, the sacred hill of Celtic gods, along with eight of his clerics. The way there was fraught with ambushes and so he cast a spell of invisibility over them; their enemies saw only eight deer.

Afterwards the "Deer's Cry" became the name of Patrick's hymn of protection, or *lorica*.

I have been known to whisper this and other *loricas* to myself as my children set out in cars or planes.

MARCH 19 ❧ WOMEN CHURCH

When I was little, women wore hats to church and weren't allowed to serve as elders. Women ministers were unknown. Although women could be deaconesses, missionaries, or nuns, the robes and stoles – the power of the priesthood, the power of the Word – belonged to men.

Now women can be ministers, at least in most Protestant denominations. The jargon and the rituals belong to us as well.

We should be careful.

It was, in some ways, an asset to be powerless. We refrained from religious jargon because we hadn't gone to theological school, and we didn't know the codes. We couldn't talk over people's heads and we never, never could assume that being able to say *eschatological* or *hermeneutic* helped us to know God.

We confined our activities to the kitchen, where the phrase *justification by faith* was never heard and all activity was dedicated to the sacred task of feeding the hungry.

My own priest is a woman. She uses no jargon to obscure the truth. She is at home in the kitchen as well as in the pulpit. She loves our sacred earth with pagan passion and wears her priestly robe with humble grace.

I rejoice in her wisdom and carefulness.

MARCH 20 ❧ RAIN

At night, I wake up and hear rain. I lie still and listen as long as I can, because this is a healing sound. Then Jim and I struggle out of bed and close windows, wiping down damp sills with a towel before falling back into bed.

Sometimes, if we are lucky, the wind is clearly from one direction. We can leave the windows open on the lee side of the house and let the rain whisper us back to sleep.

I hope we never have to buy an air conditioner. It would shut out the sound of wind and rain.

MARCH 21 ❧ SPRING EQUINOX AND GREEN ROOFS

Today in northern latitudes is the spring equinox, when night and day are of equal length. Sort of. It's complicated. Easter will fall on the first Sunday of the first full moon after this date. Sort of. It's also complicated. You have to be alert.

But a festival that is tied to nature (the moon) reminds us of our inextricable ties to the natural world. It is easy to forget that we are creatures of Mother Earth when springtime can seem like an assault. In my area, melting snow from asphalt-coated streets pours toxic, salty runoff down storm drains and creates an overflow of sewage into the lake.

Today is a good day to list the ways we are learning to be more gentle. It's a good day to celebrate green roofs (a flat roof fitted with a tough membrane, topped with soil and plants) and rain gardens (little collections of tough native plants at runoff sites, like the edges of parking lots or the ends of downspouts). Both of these inventions slow down runoff and prevent flooded storm drains. They're cheaper and better than more technological methods of control.

Any day that we work with nature instead of against her is worth celebrating.

MARCH 22 ❧ SWEETMAN'S GARDEN:
PRESERVING THE COMMONS

To be an elder is to make time to support heroes like my friend Adelaide. I became a green activist three years ago when she appeared at my door, visibly upset, and said, "They're going to build houses on Murray's garden."

The place she referred to is about two acres of reclaimed railway right-of-way; an idiosyncratic, abundant, gorgeous collection of apple trees and iris, rudbeckia and roses, day lilies and phlox. Children climb the apple trees and hide in the cedar hedge. Murray Sweetman created the garden over half a century, hence Sweetman's garden. People get married there, have wedding photos taken, picnic, sit and read, paint, take pictures. It is a remarkable oasis in the middle of our small northern city.

But some time after the CNR had sold its considerable right-of-way lands to our city for a dollar, city council decided to bull-doze the garden and sell the land to a developer.

So Adelaide and a lot of other people learned the agonizing art of standing in their way. We learned to be irritating to the pro-development council of that day. We learned how to leaflet, walking up and down city streets for hours dropping notices and pamphlets into mailboxes. We learned how to research and de-liver speeches – many, many speeches – at City Hall. We wrote letters to editors, lobbied councillors, and attended strategy meetings. We learned our city's official plan, especially its parks plan, inside out and backwards.

Three years later, we are slowing down the sweep of public land – the commons – into private ownership. So far, Sweet-man's garden remains. In the last election the bulldozer-prone council was replaced with a more balanced one. Murray Sweet-man, in his eighties, still weeds and prunes.

The children still surprise us by jumping out of hiding places in the hedge.

MARCH 23 ❧ SWEETMAN'S GARDEN:
MENDING THE WORLD

For this elder, saving a little place of beauty is not just a matter of green activism. It is a sacred task. We are called by God to be *Mending the World*, in the words of a church-committee-born report of that name. The fact that we cannot ever fully succeed makes the task no less holy.

Further, we are called to form partnerships with people of other faiths or no faiths, in order to protect Creation. That's what our church governors agreed to, with that report, and oh, I love them for it.

So the outreach committee of our congregation hosted a day in Sweetman's garden, erecting a huge tent just outside it and inviting painters and poets and photographers to address the crowds of nature lovers. The sun shone, and the people who love the garden were energized. A fertile boggy place of gorgeous bloom survives to bless our city.

MARCH 24 ❧ TOMATO MIRACLES

The world would be more mended if there were more gardens. Picture a world in which we all could pick our own ripe tomatoes in the summer. Even if we had only a balcony we could plant, say, tomatoes in pots.

We could watch the miracle of the tomato plant, watered and fed, growing toward the sun. One day it sprouts little yellow flowers. We could pinch off the little side shoots that want to grow between the main stem and the branches. We could tie the plants to stakes, using our old pantyhose. Although elders seldom wear pantyhose (one of the perks of eldership is living every day in blue jeans) someone younger and less fortunate could gift us theirs. And we could water and feed, water and feed.

And then one day we would eat a tomato right off the vine. Our own tomato, a descendant of the one from Montezuma's garden that began it all.

Our very own tomatoes, warm and sweet from the sun. We would share them with the neighbours because tomatoes always overproduce. We would visit over spaghetti sauce and agree to share zucchini next summer. We would plot the end of world hunger.

It's not too late. We could start a plant from seed, today, in a sunny window.

MARCH 25 ❧ DEPRESSION

How to beat depression. Oh, not the bone-deep sadness that has no reason to it, which we call *clinical* and have learned to treat with drugs and careful words. But ordinary sadness, the kind that has a cause: a friend who's moved away, some loss that's not too deep to heal with time and care, a grandchild living far away.

Make bread. Get out the bowl and pour in water – not too hot – and add some yeast and honey, and then some flour. Whole wheat, because this bread signals wholeness. Knead it for a long, long time, till you remember what your hands have always known, that health and goodness come from well-loved work.

Let it rise. It is a miracle. Punch it down, and let it rise again, this time in pans.

You too will rise again. Remember.

Now bake until the loaves are high and golden. Turn them out to grace your kitchen with the smell of life your grandmother knew, and your great-grandmother, and all the mothers before them.

You come from strong women. Remember.

Take a loaf, still hot, and join a friend. There's happiness in this.

MARCH 26 ❧ SIMPLE WHOLE WHEAT BREAD

> 2 teaspoons yeast
> 3 cups lukewarm water
> 2 tablespoons honey
> 7 or 8 cups whole wheat flour
> ½ teaspoon salt
> 2 tablespoons canola oil

In a large bowl, dissolve the yeast in water, add the honey, mix, and let stand for about ten minutes. Mix together 4 cups flour and the salt in another bowl. Gradually beat this into the yeast mixture. Beat in the oil. Mix in as much of the remaining flour as you can, then flour your work surface generously and turn the dough out onto it. Knead, adding any remaining flour as you go. The dough will be sticky. You will have to knead for about 15 minutes, and it will still be slightly sticky, not as smooth as white bread.

Round up, put in an oiled bowl, cover with a tea towel, and let rise in a warm place until doubled in size, between one and two hours. (I usually put the dough on a rack over a sink of hot water, or into an oven that has been heated slightly and then turned off.)

Punch down, and let rise again in the oiled bowl about an hour. Turn out onto a floured work surface, shape into two balls, and put each one into a well-oiled loaf pan to rise again, about 25 minutes. If you like, before this last rising, you can mix one egg with two tablespoons of water, brush this onto the loaves, and then dust with sesame seeds.

Then bake for 55 minutes at 350°F until the loaves are brown and sound hollow if you tap them. Remove from pans (you'll need a sharp knife) and cool on a rack.

NOTE: *I like this so much that I usually multiply the recipe by four, and freeze some of the resulting eight loaves. If you don't have a large oven, or a convection oven, you might have to let half the dough rise a third time while you bake four of the loaves. This won't hurt, although when you do get the remaining dough shaped into loaves, they will rise very quickly.*

MARCH 27 ❧ THE LANGUAGE OF LOVE

One morning we were sitting at breakfast sharing the morning newspaper, an activity that involves surreptitious stealing of coveted sections. I was just figuring out how I might grab the front section while Jim was up getting coffee when a small voice drifted down the stairs. "I'm awake now!"

It was our grandson Eli, visiting from far away, and fully embarked on his life's mission, which is to instruct anyone available in joyous living. Soon we had given up the newspaper and were pretending to be frogs, hopping around the kitchen. I don't actually hop well, but I can say *ribbet* with great enthusiasm.

Northrop Frye, one of Canada's most beloved intellectuals, referred to the gospels as the "language of love." I agree. The language of love tells the truth about justice for aboriginal people and the earth, about the yearning of humanity for its soul, about the absolute priority of children. It is what is spoken by our grandson, rushing down the stairs so we can leap about saying *ribbet* while our porridge cools.

The gospels may be larger than we thought.

MARCH 28 ❧ A PRAYER FOR EARLY SPRING

Bless the melting ice
And bless the heaps of snow, surrounded now by grass.
Bless the shiny rocks
And bless the skinny leaves of crocus, trembling in the breeze.
Oh, bless the purple after winter white
Bless the meager tips of green, the cautious haze of apple buds,
My husband sweeping sand onto the street,
And bless the blizzard come to blast our hearts into humility.
Amen.

MARCH 29 ❧ THE WORLD AT SIX

We are all connected with the world at large, the whole round earth jam-packed with humans. But sometimes our health advisors suggest we turn off the news. It is too much, it is making us sick. Take a news break, they say.

That is probably good advice. The world goes on without us. We are not indispensable. The Prime Minister makes decisions without our input. But who will demand an accounting from those leaders allowing damage to the earth, if not us?

MARCH 30 ❧ MYSTERY STORIES

As an elder I don't accomplish as much I used to, and that seems to be all right. At least in winter, my inner cop has stopped saying, "Get something done! Right now!"

It's a relief.

So most winter evenings I stretch out on the couch in front of the fire with a murder mystery. This is not productive. I usually read about half a book in a couple of hours. (Yes, I used to make a living out of words, and I can't stop reading like lightning.)

My little wood-smoke-scented-idyll requires a couple of trips a week to the library. I walk in order to counteract all this couch time.

But I wonder why mysteries are so seductive. The appeal might be the mystery's narrative shape: a terrible death creates chaos into which a hero, usually badged, ventures out in order to – eventually – restore order and harmony in the world. Or it might be the characters: the hero is flawed, but seldom tragically, and has redeeming traits including persistence. The villain is usually recognizably, comfortingly, a villain, unlike in real life where the bad guys are, well, a lot like you and me.

Even when I succumb to a mad desire for the latest adventure of a well-loved protagonist and actually *buy* the book, I comfort myself. This is the imposition of pattern and design on a muddled world. This is not extravagance, it is therapy.

But perhaps it's good that spring has come at last.

MARCH 31 ❧ OBEDIENCE

On a bad day, create beauty. Work in a garden, any garden; a balcony window box will do. Or paint a room in something sunshine-coloured. Plant a tree, surreptitiously on public land if necessary.

You will think this advice is trite, and maybe that is so. It reeks of "forget yourself and live for others," or "get moving and you'll feel better," and other things friends say when they find your distress uncomfortable.

But beauty demands obedience. While this is an attribute I don't much like when it is requested of me by humans, beauty-as-master has no armies. We obey its dictates only because we want to, even if we are sad or tired.

The result of serving beauty is a little transformation in us and in the world. That jolt to the heart we feel when something (it could be anything from a building to a chair to a garden) has proper proportion and colour – when it's just *right* – is felt by others. We can take a camera and seek out pleasing images, and give them to friends. We can dig and seed a guerrilla garden and gratify passers-by anonymously. Our eyes (and others' eyes) will become accustomed to the pleasing play of light and shade. And beauty will have converts, more and more of them, until the whole world rises up and revolts against treeless expanses of concrete and says, "No more."

Pretty good work for a bad day.

APRIL 1 ❧ APRIL FOOL'S DAY

The best April Fool's joke I ever encountered ran in a magazine called *The Saturday Review* sometime in the late 1960s. Our family was living in the United States, and our meagre student budget included a subscription to this thoughtful literary magazine.

One issue carried a succinct but enthusiastic piece on a move to create much-needed social housing by expropriating golf courses. This article drew a feast of vociferous letters. I don't have the correspondence in front of me (it was 40 years ago) but I am pretty sure that most of them were dead set against such a project. None of the letter writers had noticed that the issue in question was dated April 1. The editors quickly ran a selection of these letters, along with a note essentially shouting April Fool!

But now I am an elder like many of those long-ago *Saturday Review* letter writers, dignified and financially secure enough to belong to a golf club if I wished. I need to remember this story. While there's no danger I will ever want to spend time hitting a small ball with a big stick, I am extremely attached to my dignity.

April Fool's Day exists to make sure that I and other elders don't forget the art of laughing at our odd little human ways.

APRIL 2 ❧ PERSEPHONE

This is the time of year to rediscover the old Greek gods, the ones you haven't thought of since high school. The more we understand the Christian narrative as a powerful mix of history and myth – albeit a myth that serves essential truth – the freer we are to see the significance of other stories.

For instance, Persephone's capture, while picking flowers in the sun, by the god of the underworld who "caught her up reluctant on his golden car and bare her away lamenting" (in the words of Hesiod). Nobody achieves maturity and wisdom unless we journey down, like Persephone, into our own dark unconscious.

But all around us that story is unfolding once again, just as the poet Homer described. The flowers Persephone picked ("crocuses and beautiful violets, irises also and hyacinths and the narcissus which Earth made to grow at the will of Zeus") are blooming in our gardens. Persephone's mother, pacing and furious since her daughter disappeared, has relented and allowed the earth to bloom again. The journey of return from the heart of winter has been safely undertaken once more.

It's not so different from the story of Jesus, entombed in the earth after his death and then called back to life while the ones who loved him rejoiced.

The light of spring is illumination enough for an elder to consider what part of us needs to return to life. Our laughter? Our willingness to risk failure? Perhaps our humility?

APRIL 3 ❧ MANAGING POLITICIANS

It's very important, when seeking to influence city hall, to have the artists on board. They have the vision you require.

Artist Liz Lott has done a painting of the downtown of our city. Right down the middle of the main street she has placed a perfect row of healthy pine trees, making the whole urban landscape a mix of forest and city.

People viewing the artwork are captivated, and ask, "When was *that* there?"

It never was. And it never will be, unless an artist imagines it first.

APRIL 4 ❧ PADDLING WITH MY YOUNG DAUGHTER

There are nests on the cliff
Look for dark V's, she commands
That's how you find them.
Bluebells against the rockred lichen
her yellow jacket
love's colours hurt my eyes.

White flowers float rooted in black mud

princess of the lilies paddles
into her garden
aerial hordes of swallows, fork-tailed, rise

merganser navy churns
she nods and
a thousand frogs rise on tiny webbed feet and
wave webbed fingers
faces raised

one kiss
skin splits toes wiggle hands stretch and curve

See. She makes herself a prince.

APRIL 5 ❧ MODERN WOMEN

Now that women can become ministers and doctors, lawyers and members of parliament, we'd better not forget how to be shaman and witch. Every profession has its jargon and the net effect, if we are not careful, is to disconnect us from the earth.

We need to be priests who remember how to speak of God without codes, doctors who respect green medicine, lawyers who see both grace and judgment in the law's beauty, and legislators who understand that children are the most important.

Today's children, and children fifty years from now, will require clean water and wild areas to play in. It is a simple concept, no jargon required: they are all the children of God.

APRIL 6 ❧ GREENSPACE

I have almost become used to appearing at city council, even though I am tense beforehand, and have to write out every word I plan to say. Our GreenSpace group – a loose coalition of organizations and individuals all equally horrified by the potential sale of much-loved public lands – has made presentations again and again.

I am becoming more accustomed to an ambivalent reception from some city staff. All this agitation makes their working lives more difficult. They are caught between an unhappy public and members of a determined council.

But my main discomfort now, as a "green" activist, is my body's inability to keep up the pace. I want to weed the garden we fought to save, and plant trees at the lake, and dig in my own treasured garden, and I can't quite do it all.

This is not an issue with my fellow tree-huggers. Everyone is happy that each of us does what we can. So what is it? Pride? ("I can still do this!") Guilt? ("Am I just lazy?")

Neither pride nor guilt is a useful emotion, especially for elder women.

APRIL 7 ❧ DREAMS OF HOUSES

When doing dream work it's important to be able to live with ambiguity. We never learn the full meaning of every dream. Dreams involving houses are especially difficult, because they often refer to our whole inner being. Most of us want to avoid facing our own internal flaws.

So the fact that I am not entirely sure of the meaning of the dream below might indicate I am not ready to deal with it. Dreams only tell us what we are strong enough to bear.

I dreamed someone redecorated our living room. It had big beams and pale wood and panelling, already stained in spots. Then the walls were equipped with permanent videos of western scenes, some quite violent, called Saddle Creek, Willow Creek, etc. You could turn and see a different scene of cowboy life in every direction.

Also, I seemed to be in bed and an aunt – a younger Aunt Millie, perhaps – was coming out to make breakfast. Another young woman was there and she put on a strange costume.

Another interior decorator came in and she was surprised that the beams were new. I didn't have the bill yet, but it must be very expensive.

It seems my inner life is changing (the "redecoration"). But there might be a "beam" in my eye that I am ignoring. Some character "stains," some strong ("violent") inner conflicts remain. These could be related to my being a "cowboy" instead of a team player.

It is time to wake up ("breakfast") aided by two young aspects of my psyche/soul ("Aunt Millie" and "another young woman"). The latter stands for a new ("strange") *persona* on my part. (*Persona* is simply the mask we put on for the various roles we play in life. When I host a party, I wear my domestic goddess persona. Lightly, I hope. When I am a reporter, I wear my reporter role. Et cetera.)

This might refer to the fact that retirement – or being an elder – is still a new role for me.

Dreams use repetition to try to get the point across. So, again, the internal shift ("another interior decorator") and the "beams." It looks as if I am being too judgmental about something or somebody. Although the effects of this are not yet felt (the "bill"), this flaw is likely to be costly.

APRIL 8 ❧ FILL THE GAPS

Perhaps when we were little someone said we couldn't sing. Someone laughed at us when we danced, or accused us of being big and awkward. I remember clearly a neighbour who always called me "stupid." I was ten years old, at the top of my class, and he thought it made a funny nickname.

It didn't.

My children think it is time I said goodbye to that 58-year-old memory.

So someone said you can't write poetry. Say goodbye to that someone. Write a poem. Eldership is about filling in life's spaces with the things you thought you couldn't do.

Poetry is not paragliding. It has no risk attached.

APRIL 9 ✳ HOW TO SLEEP

When I mutter about not sleeping well, people respond with the dictum that older people just don't sleep as much. But I'd rather not lie awake. I'd rather wake up full of new energy. So:

Maybe my lying-awake worrying is trying to grab the attention I don't give it during the day. I am going to keep paper and pen close at hand so I can make a list of worries that surface at 2:00 a.m. or thereabouts. Once acknowledged, they might let me sleep.

Maybe exercise is what's missing. I am going to walk every day. Having finally come to accept that I am irrevocably task-oriented, I am finding destinations. The library, a two-mile round trip. A supermarket, also two miles, with the return carrying weights, called groceries, for extra benefit. The post office.

That should do it, along with hot milk (which makes my children scream with laughter) and a detective novel (which displaces any worried personal narrative I have for one so much worse that I forget my own).

One of the advantages of eldership is the time to do research (on sleep, for instance) and experiment, even on ourselves. If we solve this, we'll be famous.

APRIL 10 ❧ BERRY PICKING

We took Eli to Manitoulin Island and set out for a walk along the gravel road. There were butterflies and buttercups and Joe-pye weed growing in the ditches. "I want," said our little grandson, "to go to a museum."

His life has been spent in cities. So we showed him how to tell if someone likes butter (hold a buttercup under their chin and peer carefully for the yellow reflection) and how to make daisy chains. We found bees gathering pollen and a groundhog hole and ducks gathering on the bay. We jumped from rock to rock, pretending all else was ocean filled with sharks. We found raspberries growing by the side of the road and ate them from our hands.

Soon he had utterly forgotten about museums. But we were just in time. Children need nature, unmediated by parks, glorious and necessary though the latter may be.

Children need berry picking. My father picked blueberries, and expected us all to help. We did. My mother made sweet blue syrup studded with berries, which we ate all winter with toast or pancakes. She made pies. We understood from this that the land will feed us; that, despite flies and bee stings and winter cold, the land loves us dearly.

Our grandchildren need to know this too.

APRIL 11 ❧ HEALING

One of the best ways to heal ourselves when we are wounded emotionally is with physical movement, preferably purposeful. In fact, I think that may be one of the ways we survive the trauma of moving and leaving beloved friends behind. We lift boxes. We move furniture. We climb on chairs and hang pictures. We clean.

All this makes us very tired, and so we sleep.

Eventually, most things are in place. We feel – accomplished. Time passes. And we notice one day that we feel better.

APRIL 12 ❧ PRAYER

Today I believe in God
outrageous force driving tulips up and up
every blossom righteous.

I believe in the wisdom of my apple tree, tiny cells doubling and re-doubling making leaves and blooms and eventual small fruit ready already for the fall, in April, yet.

I believe in bees and also in the foolish hopeful robin who tries to nest on a flat spot above my front door and all the twigs and little bits of grass fall into my mailbox. Where does she go then, poor soul, to lay her eggs?

I believe in melting ice and eager joyous fishers, pulling in the ice huts and pulling out their boats.

I believe in life everlasting.
Amen.

APRIL 13 ❧ A WOMAN ELDER – LUCY AFFLECK

In 1929, Lucy Affleck was a young teacher at the United Church's Round Lake Residential School for Native children, in Stockholm, Saskatchewan. She had been there for only two months when she wrote an impassioned letter to the church's Superintendent of Indian Missions. "The children lack completely the mothering that only one could give them who lived close enough to them to know their individual dispositions," she said. "The discipline they are receiving is not the result of training or the rule of love."

In a group in which tuberculosis is rampant, there was still no heat in October, and "they are still wearing their summer clothing, the boys without underwear of any kind...there is no care to prevent serious colds."

Bathtubs don't work and the boys have to bathe in laundry tubs; toilets don't flush, and "sweeping in the boys dormitory... you will know what a dust an unoiled floor makes...is done seven days in the week by four girls, three of whom are from families with bad TB records."

What really upset her was that the prayers they learned were "meaningless... All the religious knowledge these little Indians get is a matter of form only. Of a gospel of love and light they hear nothing."

She described the poor food, the overcrowding, the principal selling apples to the children when he knew they had money from their parents.

She sent off her letter. A few weeks later she was called to the principal, who said "Your cheque is there on the desk, the truck will take you to Whitewood tomorrow."

She asked if there was any explanation.

"None, except the church demands the immediate dismissal of any one disloyal to the staff."

"In nothing that I have said or done have I been disloyal to the children or the school," Lucy said. "I reported only conditions that should not exist, and reported them to the proper authorities."

"You may take either a morning or an afternoon train," he said.

Lucy lost her job, in the depression. She was not yet thirty.

We who are retired and have no job to lose have no reason to keep silent when we see conditions that should not exist.

APRIL 14 ❧ QUICK HOT CROSS BUNS

1 cup lukewarm water
1 tablespoon dry yeast
2 tablespoons sugar
2¼ cups flour (all-purpose)
½ teaspoon salt
1½ teaspoons cinnamon
½ teaspoon nutmeg
1 egg
2 tablespoons butter (soft)
½ cup currants
¼ cup chopped citron

In a large bowl, dissolve yeast in the water. Add sugar and stir. Add 1 cup flour, the salt and the spices to yeast mixture. Beat until smooth with wooden spoon. Add egg and butter. Mix in remaining flour, currants, and citron, and beat again.

Cover with tea towel and let rise in a warm place. (I place it on a rack over hot water, or in a slightly warmed oven that has been turned off.)

Oil 12 large muffin cups. Stir down dough and spoon into muffin cups. Let dough rise again in a warm place until it reaches the top of the muffin cups, about 20 minutes.

Bake at 400°F until golden brown, about 15 to 20 minutes.

Make a cross on top of each one with simple white icing (add a little milk to some icing sugar until it is spreadable).

APRIL 15 ❧ THE WISDOM OF AGE

Some of the people who go to church or synagogue to observe the holy days of this time of year – Passover, Good Friday, Easter – are old enough to remember when the shape of the year was based on life and death and life again, and the shape of each week included Sabbath time.

That shape is less universal now. But these elders are not dead yet. People in their seventies and eighties are as alive as those in their twenties. And in a time of transition like this one, elders fulfill the function that monks of another time did. They keep memory alive. Even in the Dark Ages, says editor and commentator Martin Marty, there was "still holiness in the lives of men and women who rose above the limits of their times ...[They] could at the same time distinguish themselves for research and the routine copying of ancient manuscripts, and for cultivating a language of devotion with a simple but mystical bent that survives to our day."

I'm not suggesting that we should copy manuscripts. But we need to mark such loyalty carefully. The time will come when God will speak to us, offering a vision. And when that happens we will need someone who remembers how God's voice sounds.

APRIL 16 ❧ OLD STORIES

Humans love connection. Across the centuries or across continents, which is why we like to stay at bed-and-breakfasts, sitting around a common table as if we were a family sharing the morning meal. Or why on airplanes we delight in odd links with total strangers, like the woman on a Victoria flight who recognized my haircut and knew immediately what city I was from.

My grandson's other grandparents came to visit us in winter, from southern California. They have become our friends, connected with us through the shared joy of grandparenting.

Although Karen and Bill, Jim and I are linked by one small boy, there is no English word for that connection. There is however, one in Hebrew. As Karen explained, we are *machatonim*, the co-grandparents who preside over the formation of a new generation.

It is an enduring connection which we love.

APRIL 17 ❧ GIFTS

Long ago I answered the door one morning to find my friend holding out a huge bunch of asparagus from her garden. Without thinking I said, "Don't you need that?"

Her face fell.

Just recently, we had all been together to dance in the lovely space of her newly raised barn and celebrate the fact that no cows had been in the old one when it burned. My husband, her minister, had comforted her family the night the old barn burned, and had blessed the new one the day it was complete. She wanted to do a kindness in return.

I never made that mistake again. At that door I received brimming pitchers of maple syrup and newly divided perennials. I was given fresh-picked fiddleheads from a forever secret source. I learned to make very light biscuits so that I would have something to give in return.

Many things can bind people together: war, a common enemy, gossip, fear. But I prefer it to be the gifts of our abundance.

APRIL 18 ❧ NEIGHBOURHOODS

I believe in the importance of liveable, breathable and, above all, walkable neighbourhoods with neighbourhood schools. People get to know each other as parents of children attending the same school. They greet each other when they are walking or shopping, or at the movies.

Because the families know each other, the children can play more safely in the streets. Because the children can walk to school, they are physically more active and healthy. Because each of the children lives in the "village that is required to raise a child," everyone pitches in to offer them a more complete education.

Space for common work and play is good too. Many children

in my neighbourhood have learned to seed and weed and love the flowers in Sweetman's garden.

This keeps us all healthy, body and soul.

APRIL 19 ❧ NATIVE SPIRITUALITY

I have walked many labyrinths, but none more powerful than one in my own church.

We gathered in a loose circle in the church gymnasium. It was evening, and dark; the only light came from a scattering of candles around the huge room. Inside the circle was a large drum with four chairs pulled up to it. Throughout the evening, whoever wished to took a turn pounding a steady rhythm set by Terry Dokis, the Ojibway elder who had brought the drum.

He had also set up an enormous labyrinth, patterned after the one found in the great cathedral in Chartres, France. The room was heavy with the scent of pine from branches surrounding this ancient design. There were carefully-composed symbols at the east, south, west, and north points of the room. Water, fire, earth, and air each had a place at one of the four directions. And people walked the labyrinth, accompanied by the calming, comforting, steadying heartbeat of the drum.

Terry has been leading a revival of interest in this pre-Christian design that was enthusiastically adopted by Christians in the Middle Ages. The labyrinth's slow, circuitous pathway inward and outward fed the mystical spirit of the age. Its intricate length provided a path, in a pilgrimage-conscious age, for those who wanted to live out their faith with their bodies by walking and praying, but couldn't go to the Holy Land.

Terry sees a strong similarity to the medicine wheel of First Nations spirituality.

The evening became a symbol of the blessings that continue to be offered to the Christian church from the First Nations. From them, our churches could receive a new heart – one that beats to a rhythm animated by a spirit springing from this side of the Atlantic. The marks of this spirit are simple but radical love for the land; a way of meeting together that listens patiently; and above all, a powerful spirituality filled with gratitude and a sense of mystery.

APRIL 20 ❧ SEEDLINGS

It is April and every window is jammed with trays full of earth and small green plants. Every morning I am up watering, spraying, checking for any little web of spores that signals disease. I am moving baby seedlings around, so that those that are too crowded have more room, and places where no seedlings sprouted are filled.

I am mother to a thousand green babies.

This is how God feels, I am sure of it.

APRIL 21 ❦ HAPPINESS

I am a perfectionist the way people in Alcoholics Anonymous are alcoholics. We struggle, and it will be so forever. The worst thing about being a perfectionist is that I often forget to be happy now. Now, before I walk into the wall that is my really old age.

In my really old age, there may be no more books with dog-eared covers to explain how much this one was loved, just little electronic tablets scrolling up and down. Will there be church? Will people sit in light that flows all coloured through stained glass? Will people sing about an infant God, and ponder what the resurrection – such a word – could mean?

I should be happy now.

APRIL 22 ❦ EARTH DAY

It's a wonderful idea and responsible for a multitude of good things, including international pressure by ordinary citizens to act on climate change. But – isn't it a bit like bringing Mom breakfast in bed on Mother's Day and letting her clean the toilets by herself the rest of the year?

Shouldn't every day be Earth Day?

APRIL 23 ❧ PANSIES

Pansies don't mind snow and frost at all. In fact, you can plant pansies outdoors in a pot anytime after the end of March if you can find a place to buy them. They will freeze at night and perk up happily as soon as the sun hits them. And their blossoms are so human-like. So friendly.

Plant out pansies. Yellow, purple, burgundy, blue. Make passers-by happy and astonished that such colour can appear in frosty weather. If we convince them of our elder magic in this simple way, they may trust us on more complex matters: new bike lanes, community gardens, a tree bylaw, traffic calming.

I have a wish list. Together, the pansies and I are strong.

APRIL 24 ❧ THE POEM OF TODAY

A very precise way to one's inner world is by writing a poem. It is why we sing poems, called hymns, in church. It is the reason we can interpret (more or less) the images found in a dream – they are the same ones found in poems and songs. Of course, no symbol is ever fully understood. That's why it is called symbolic.

So. Today, a five-minute poetry-writing workshop. You need
Paper
Pen
A timer (optional)

Take a piece of paper and write on it: "You fill my heart with love, God when…"

Now write only six more lines. No more.

No rhyme or rhythm is needed.

AND

Be economical. Use as few words as you can.

Be specific. Don't say "beautiful trees." Say "spruce" or "maple" or "ancient pine," for instance.

Set your timer for one minute. Take one minute of silence to contemplate.

Set your timer for five minutes. During that time, write down what came to you in the silence.

Put the paper aside and go on with your day.

Later, you can read your poem aloud at dinner.

APRIL 25 ❧ ICE BREAKING UP

This week the ice will go out on the lake. Already it sounds like a thousand cocktail parties, the rotten ice clinking as it falls piece by miniature piece into the water. We nose our canoe through the small ice floes, listening. It is the music of spring.

APRIL 26 ❧ WHAT MAKES A GOOD LIFE?

This is not an abstract philosophical question. It's very practical. How can you find your good life if you don't know what it is? Is it wealth? Passion for a cause? What makes a "good" cause? Is it fame? Is it contentment in obscurity, privacy, love, physical well-being, the creation of beauty? Beauty in what arena? Your house? Your garden? Your city?

Is a good life one that you concoct, like a traditional recipe, out of this ingredient and that? A little wealth, say, a lot of education, some kindness, and a modicum of justice-seeking.

Can one even hope for a good life, given the unforeseeable – illness, brain chemistry, a stray car on the freeway one morning? But what is life without hope?

Everyone talks about the balanced life. Aristotle thought this was a good thing, and called it the golden mean. I suspect the good life involves giving your whole heart to something you value passionately, even if it will not be granted in your lifetime.

My elder passion is a good earth for my grandchild and his peers.

APRIL 27 ❧ THE FOUNDING FAMILY

Y ou won't forget the founding children, said one of our grown-up offspring when his nephew was born. He was referring to his siblings and himself, and he was joking, of course. Nobody could be less interested in a family dynasty, nor more enslaved to our first grandchild than him.

We all hasten to protect the youngest. This is the way the world should be: the most vulnerable, the children, are the most important.

And he doesn't know what the parents of grown children know. That when we look at them, we see and love not only the competent adult but the terrified child on the first day of school and the determined ten-year-old on the diving board.

We won't forget. The founding children are ever-young, as long as their elders are alive.

APRIL 28 ❧ THE ROAD TO EMMAUS

I love the biblical account of Jesus walking with two of his disciples soon after he has risen from the dead. They don't recognize him. Well, why would they? He has died, after all.

But then, as they walk and talk, the two disciples, Cleopas and an unnamed one, somehow end up speaking in unison: "They said, 'Stay with us...'"

It makes me believe these two disciples were a married couple, so long accepted as having one agreed-upon opinion that even direct quotes are attributed to "them."

Maintaining one's own identity in a long relationship seems to have been an issue even two thousand years ago. Not that I am alarmed. Marriage is always a slow dance between loss of identity and strict autonomy, between dependence and independence or – some suggest – interdependence. If you marry early, some parts of your identities are liable to fuse. This sometimes makes life easier and sometimes much more difficult.

Just don't imagine that the dance becomes less complex when you are an elder, or any less wonderful. Life would be incredibly boring if you always agreed, especially when retirement throws you together for longer periods of time.

But it's not too late to seek counselling if by now you have not yet learned to differ respectfully.

APRIL 29 ❧ CAMPFIRES

I know that we should not confuse climate and weather. Climate is the long-term trend, weather happens now.

But it seems that summer after summer, for many years, a fire ban is in place whenever we are canoeing. It has become difficult to build a campfire in order to make pancakes and bacon and eggs and stew and bread in the bush. Of course we have our tiny propane burner, but it is hard to regulate and the pancakes stick.

If we can't build a campfire, how will we teach our grandson that the land loves him; that he is strong and can live in that love? How will we tell him stories of his great-grandfather who knew (the legend goes) how to survive in the bush, supplied with only matches and a fishhook?

It should be mandatory for climate change skeptics to spend a few summers canoeing.

APRIL 30 ❧ ELI AND THE GINGERBREAD COOKIES

Eli has a favourite book called *Gingerbread Friends* by children's writer Jan Brett. He doesn't actually own this book. A friend loans us her copy whenever he is in town or we get it from the library.

Last July when he was here we read, as always, the story of the little gingerbread boy who is lonely, but is gifted at the end with a huge (pop-out) party attended by many friends.

"Do we have eggs, Nana?" Eli asked after we had read it. "Do we have flour? Do we have ginger and butter and molasses?"

Soon we were making cookies in a cinnamon-scented kitchen, despite the July heat and Nana's ironclad rule that cooking in the summer is done on the barbecue.

I wonder what Eli learns from this book. That libraries are good? That you can make friends (and eat them?). That many things can be found in books, including a reflection of our own circumstances and directions for making cookies? Maybe he absorbs a sense of permanence. *Gingerbread Friends* has been a constant in his life since before he could talk.

I know what I learn: that I am in charge of making memories. That I must listen well, with an ear for what cannot be articulated but lies beneath the words.

I hope when my grandson is old, the smell of ginger and cinnamon will make him think of his Nana, and he will remember how he was loved.

MAY 1 ❧ BELTANE

My Celtic grandmother was psychic. She would often know when someone was going to call. She dreamed of bad events (a fire, for instance) before they happened, and with that knowledge could sometimes prevent them.

Or so the family lore goes. Her name was Mary Duncan (I called her Barney), and she came to Canada on her own as a teenager from Elgin, Scotland. She was a fine bread maker and a gentle, infinitely kind grandmother. For a time, when I was an awkward preadolescent and needed company, we played canasta after school every day.

I am very proud of her, proud to be a Celt.

In Scotland and Ireland during pagan times, May 1 was a time of pilgrimage to the holy wells. Offerings were made. The spirit of the water was honoured. After Christianization, churches were built over many of the wells and water that the priest had blessed became the only holy water.

It is time for the Celtic tradition to be rediscovered, and the spirit of the water honoured. Industries that damage sacred water (which is all water), should be prosecuted severely. Like my psychic grandmother who could sense danger – she awoke, shouting, when my father had a fatal heart attack – we should face the coming peril and throw into a well any CEO or citizen who heedlessly – by toxic chemicals or sheer extravagance – harms the water.

MAY 2 &c TODAY, AT MY DESK

My cave beneath the house
Is full of darkness and
I hide.

I grow stories here.
They feed on my soul to live.

But soon the freshness will come, soon the sun, even here.
I know this from my father.

Life finds light. Branches, pruned, thicken and green.

MAY 3 &c SCRIPTURE

The Bible is full of strange events and sometimes awful images. Like the fate of Judas, one of the twelve respected people who travelled with Jesus and an elder by any definition.

Judas ended up hemorrhaging to death in a field after he was handed his notorious thirty pieces of silver. But why is Judas, who was only doing what scripture said he must, an object of loathing and condemned to die from a biblical version of Ebola?

The complicated questions make scripture worth studying. Scripture is open-ended, puzzling, ambiguous, contradictory, metaphorical, often beautiful, and frequently brutal. It requires interpretation, not literal acceptance. But taken as a whole, it conveys a universe in which compassion is the ultimate goal. Loving one another is the way we get there.

The Bible is a long story about love that never ignores the fact of evil.

MAY 4 ❧ AN ELDER'S SMALL PLEASURES

I am cleaning a glass table, completely different from my own loved old pine one. Who would have thought I would enjoy something so foreign. But eldership is a long voyage into a far country. I know that, armed with my bottle of Windex (familiar) and my son's shiny steel and glass table (unfamiliar).

I have learned to love the way it shimmers and makes every meal a party.

MAY 5 ❧ NOT YOUR FAULT

There is no way around it. Aging hurts. The older we get, the more arthritis creeps into our lives, attacking whatever parts of our bodies we employed to make a living. I have a friend who was a bricklayer, and his back hurts. I sat at a computer and my neck hurts.

Experts say that if you have used your body properly, it shouldn't hurt. I say that eventually your body notices what you are doing anyway, and retaliates.

When my mother began to hurt, and told me about it, I did my best to ignore it. (This was not my best self in action.) She would demand to be taken to various doctors and they did their best, but some pain you can't fix.

I always felt she was blaming me for that. But now that I have begun to hurt in my own fashion, I realize that what I experienced as blame was just discomfort on her part, and fear of more discomfort.

Moral: Eventually, you will have to manage some tenacious ache or other, balancing painkillers with the side-effects they produce. It's the price of a long life. Try to talk about it at length only with your doctor and the mirror, because it makes the people you love hurt when they see you in pain. Above all, be sure to tell any caregivers or children who notice this that you know they have done everything in their power to fix this, and you are grateful.

Above all, don't tell them it will happen to them some day. Why spoil the surprise?

MAY 6 ❧ STUDIES

Ever since someone did a study that showed coffee was good for you (yes, I did read that… somewhere), I have dreamed of other studies. Lying on the couch reading novels all day is good for you. Food eaten after midnight has no calories.

My children tell me that in their early years I shoved them outside whenever the weather was good, and often when it wasn't, lecturing them on the well-researched virtues of fresh air. Now, grown up, on a fine day they have trouble sitting at a desk. The moral imperative singing through their brains is "Get outside! Right now! Don't waste the sunshine!"

I am not terribly athletic myself. So it does make me wonder how much anxious reading by parents of this or that new study is propelled by the hope that our children will be what we are not, that they will be *better* than ourselves.

If we could only define *better*, someone could do a study on the question.

MAY 7 ❦ MONTREAL

Somehow I have begun to love cities, after a lifetime of being faintly suspicious of crowds and density and close living. Cities are built, after all, by God's beloved creatures, just like beaver dams and anthills.

I especially love Montreal, even though I have to struggle mightily to understand what is being said to me in French. I have a grandson there. Perhaps my newfound affection for crowded sidewalks and off-beat restaurants just goes to show that doors can open even in my hard heart, if he pushes on them.

And I have discovered that everyone doesn't have to live in a single-family detached house. Oh no. Multiple family dwellings are fine. A place up a flight of stairs or two offers access to the wonders of the city: tree-lined streets and ample parks and learning how to live gently so you don't disturb others a floor below. To my surprise, all this is fine. Just fine.

It is possible to cross from one culture to another, even if you don't speak the language. Love helps.

MAY 8 ❧ SARAH

God also said to Abraham, "As for Sarai your wife, you are no longer to call her Sarai; her name will be Sarah. I will bless her and will surely give you a son by her. I will bless her so that she will be the mother of nations; kings of peoples will come from her."

Abraham fell facedown; he laughed and said to himself, "Will a son be born to a man a hundred years old? Will Sarah bear a child at the age of ninety?" (Genesis 17:15–17 NIV)

Some believe that dreams are a gift of God. So as elders, when we have a dream or vision in which a baby appears, we need to take it seriously. Abraham had a lot of difficulty restraining his mirth, even when he knew he had been talking with God.

In the story, it turned out that Sarah *did* have a child. He was so beloved that he was called Isaac, or laughter.

It is never too late, such a dream says to us, for something new to come into your life. For you to have a new idea, begin a new project, become in some strange way a new person.

It is the nature of dreams to be bizarre. But they may signal newness of life.

MAY 9 ❧ ALZHEIMER'S SPIRITUALITY

A friend has dementia. I'll call her Mona. She is one of the fortunate ones: her husband adores her and looks after her with patience and compassion. A daughter has moved to be close to her parents and offers respite. My friend is further blessed with a next-door neighbour who is a model of organized kindness – it's the only way I can express it – someone who plans her life so she can be unobtrusively, tactfully kind to others. "I'll just go and sit with Mona at lunch," this neighbour says to me quietly. "She still knows who I am."

At an event after church yesterday, Mona wanted to dance to the music. My husband, who was there, says he wanted to sit and soak in the spirituality of the excellent presentation.

But he knew to pay gentle attention to Mona, because he is a compassionate man by nature. And also, I think, because in our little church community we have all been taught – by a good husband and a kind neighbour – how to be with people who were once bright and lively and now are a little lost. We have learned what is important.

When people ask what use church is, this story would be one answer.

MAY 10 ❧ THE RESURRECTION

What do we do when someone integral to our lives is gone? I remember our first spring as a family after my father died. I drove two hours north to clean up and plant what was now my mother's garden. There were his tulips, marching steadfastly the entire length of the yard, mute crimson witnesses to my father's continued presence.

More recently, there were the tears Jim and I shed out on the Trans-Canada Highway, just outside of Thunder Bay. We had stopped to see the statue of a frail, weary Terry Fox placed approximately where his run across the country came to an end. I am always crazily proud to tell non-Canadian relatives that Canada's national hero is a one-legged young marathoner who died before he could reach his own finish line, breaking twenty-five million hearts in the process.

Fox is a powerful symbol of resurrection as inextinguishable hope, of absolute refusal to give in to the despair that is itself a little death.

When we do Terry Fox runs, or band together as a community to run, walk, wheel, paddle, dance, or plant tulips in someone's name, we too are witnesses to resurrection.

MAY 11 ❧ MY MOTHER KNITTING

When my mother moved, resisting, into an assisted living residence, she was already 91, and blind. A staff member, Sandy, asked me what she had enjoyed doing before she lost her sight. I described her knitting, the treasured sweaters my children had worn, saved, and passed on to our grandson.

Sandy suggested I bring in some needles and wool. The day after I did that, I found my mother knitting a scarf. Her first effort was an alarming length of pale blue wool, full of holes. It was six inches wide in some places, ten or twelve in others. It was for me. I have it still. When I was annoyed with her, I would refuse to wear it (she couldn't tell, and it made me feel, childishly, better.)

She did scarves for her son-in-law and scarves for her grandchildren. Another, younger resident would mend the holes and add fringe. The colour that would suit each person best was the source of animated discussion and soon, miraculously, her knitting became accomplished. There were fewer holes and the edges were even.

Before she could get bored, her *fashionista* granddaughter suggested more colour and sufficient length to wrap around the neck several times and still hang down. This too was conquered. I was sent more frequently in search of wool, and soon my friends and the friends of friends – a whole Facebook of warmly wrapped individuals – sported very long multi-striped scarves.

We resembled aged university students who either celebrated diversity in a big way or had no idea what our college colours actually were.

My mother was happy. She was productive again, even if she couldn't see her finished work. She knit and knit until, at 94, her hands gave out and she couldn't hold the needles anymore.

It took another year. But that's when my mother, the elder who knit to keep her loved ones warm, began to die from lack of usefulness.

MAY 12 ❧ AN ELDER'S SMALL PLEASURES (TWO)

This is high season for gardening. Head filled with visions, I go round the yard planting early seeds, digging, filling pots with compost, moving and dividing perennials.

I am happy. Look at me. I can still carry heavy items. I am strong. This is a particular joy for one who is an elder, and I take note and savour and luxuriate in every precious minute of it. Non-gardeners pause and address the whirling dervish who lives in this yard. "What a lot of work!" they say wonderingly. No, it's not. It is proof of life.

MAY 13 ❧ DREAMS OF PEOPLE

When we don't actually know the people in our dreams, we can assume they are shorthand for parts of ourselves. I had this dream not long after I retired. I think the dream was asking me to face some fears I had been reluctant to acknowledge.

A small boy playing in the grass fell off into chalky water. I jumped in and pulled him out. Why did no one (else) jump in? Was the water acidic?

Then I was in a big room with other people and Oprah. But I was busy trying to get something read (or written?) and everyone was making his or her statement to Oprah. When it came to me, I made something up. Then I noticed she was sitting near me. How could I have missed my opportunity to really impress her?

Also, I was looking after a baby. I was naked from the waist up. Then I gave the baby back, feeling a little foolish about my lack of clothes, especially as I was in a big crowd, and had to walk down an aisle facing people.

A small boy could be code for some underdeveloped part of me that – like small boys – is full of adventure. The dream is pointing to my current fear that I will just dissolve (in the "acidic" water) of retirement.

My effort to "get something written" points to the same fear. How will life be with my old role of journalist gone? I may not be able to "really impress" anyone. There is still a performer in me ("Oprah") who wants to do that.

In fact the "child" – a new venture, new idea – is too young and not mine, so it has to be given back. I don't seem to have the persona required to pull it off. I have a "lack of clothes." That is awkward because I still have to face people, perhaps in the church ("aisle") where I have done most of my life's professional work.

This dream is not as depressing as it sounds. Dreams just ask us to acknowledge things we have been trying to ignore, so we can change.

MAY 14 ❧ HOW TO PRAY

My ancestors knew how to pray. A beautiful prayer from the highlands of Scotland begins,

I will kindle my fire this morning
In presence of the holy angels of heaven.[4]

My ancestors prayed many times during the day, their prayers tied to the need to light the fire or plant the vegetables or churn the milk. This kept them aware of their deep connections to both "the lowliest thing that liveth" and to God.

It is to our great pain that we have lost these powerful connections. It is not that we don't believe in God. Many people have found ways to imagine God and allow the world to be sacred even in a postmodern culture. But the rhythm of our lives has been disrupted, and we need to find new anchors to hang prayer on, since we no longer blow on the coals in the hearth in order to make breakfast.

Perhaps I could pray when I make the coffee, and again when I make the bed. I could pray when I pick up the paper from the front steps, and again when I turn on my computer. I could pray in the supermarket checkout line, silently.

As long as I can imagine the coffee farmer and the cotton-grower, the forester and the papermaker, the miner who found the resources that make up my computer and the linesperson who keeps the electricity flowing, perhaps I can connect to a living holy universe.

MAY 15 ❦ ELEVEN LEFT

It's a story about elders living two thousand years ago. After Judas died, the remaining eleven of Jesus' closest followers got together to choose a replacement.

But what's wrong with eleven?

It could have been that the little Christian community was aware of twelve as a symbolic number. There were twelve Olympian Gods, twelve months of the year, twelve signs of the Zodiac, twelve tribes of Israel; one could go on and on. But I think that the apostles weren't so much uneasy about eleven as an incomplete dozen as they were determined to repair their damaged circle. They needed to take action to make their community whole again. So they prayed hard and then they chose Matthias.

That is a very human urge, the one towards wholeness and reconciliation. Although the news of any one day might not always
lead to this conclusion, I believe that the urge towards reconciliation is stronger than the one towards destruction. The desire to
include is stronger than the desire to exclude, and the instinct towards harmony is more powerful than the instinct towards war.

You might call me a dreamer.

MAY 16 ❧ THE SHADOW

It's very helpful to get to know our unknown self. As American politician Donald Rumsfeld famously said, "There are
known knowns, and there are unknown knowns."

Those unknowns can really wear you down. A friend wrote to
me with this dream that illustrates an effort by her wise inner
self to move "an unknown" into the light.

I was in my bed, in my old bedroom, and I reached
across to the nightstand to turn on the light, and it only
came on a bit – it doesn't flicker or anything, it just turns
on very dimly, as though it were very cold or something
like that. Then I felt the presence nearby, and I was very
frightened. I told it repeatedly to stop; I was screaming
at the top of my lungs, but all I could manage/hear was
a faint whisper, as though I was hoarse. I could feel the
presence moving the covers off me, and onto the floor,

and I was trying to grab them and keep them on me, but I couldn't move. It was as though I was weighted down.

Delighted to be considered an elder, I wrote back:

Something in your inner life wishes to be uncovered. Much that is in our shadows has been forced, for a long time, to stay there. Hence your fear and your difficulty speaking. This is literally something you have difficulty talking about.

Please note: Whatever it is, it is NOT necessarily something we would now regard as terrible. Our childhood selves are sometimes very impressed by something our adult selves would think inconsequential.

Unfortunately, the impression results in some quality about that little child we once were, something that is quite wonderful or creative, getting shoved into our shadow. Maybe we are told by a Grade One teacher that we don't have a good singing voice, and all our musical juices get hidden away – that is, until our adult self feels strong enough to let them come out.

Some valuable faculty or skill or trait or aspect of yours, hidden away years ago in the interests of being "civilized," is now ready to emerge. Perhaps it is something that would be extra useful now, at this stage of your life.

The next time the dream comes along, be ready. Tell yourself before you go to bed that you will ask the dream presence who he/

she is, and what he/she wants. Just say, "Who are you, and what do you want to tell me?" Have a notebook ready to write down the answer the next morning or as soon as you recover the dream.

Remember that dreams always seek our health and wholeness. They will never tell you anything that you are not ready to hear. If this were something too difficult for you to bear, the dream would not keep recurring.

MAY 17 ❧ HEDY BARTLING

Hedy Bartling was a church worker who moved from the west coast to Lethbridge, Alberta, in order to be with interned Japanese-Canadians during World War II. To me, she is a model elder.

I interviewed her many years ago for a book I was writing on the Woman's Missionary Society of the United Church. I was impressed then. Later, a manuscript by Kaz Iwassa, one of the people she had served, came across my desk, and I was more impressed.

"Bartie, we affectionately called her," writes Iwassa. "She was an impossible person. She was indomitable, unquenchable, and irrepressible. She had her down moments, and terrible migraine headaches, but she was always there when we needed her."

Bartie was so outspoken on behalf of the interns that a plain-clothes RCMP officer was assigned to keep an eye on her all through the war. "Through Bartie," Kaz goes on, "we learned about the network of churches across Canada who were involved in lobbying on our behalf. It was then that I learned how the democratic process worked, and what hard work it is too, and what part the church could play in the political life of the country. Without a doubt, the Japanese-Canadians owe the churches for the fact they were not exiled to Japan. And it was through Bartie that I came to appreciate the worth of the church."

Bartie is typical of some elder women. They cheerfully make the authorities upset, and fight for justice even when others think they are wrong. They do the unpopular thing because they think it was right.

It's the kind of elder I try to be.

MAY 18 ❧ THE CANOE

Our green canoe was the first big item we bought as a married couple. It was made of cedar strips, with handwoven seats. We thought maybe we should keep it in the living room.

That was over forty years ago. A few years ago the gunwales were showing signs of rot, and the keel had been crushed against rock so often it was frayed like an old toothbrush. Even its smooth cedar ribs looked weary, weakened a little by time, like ourselves.

Our grown children inspected the canoe and made noises about starting a repair fund. Shamed, we loaded it on the car and took it up to the Temagami Canoe Company.

It's an ancient establishment, now as in my childhood redolent of cedar and filled with marvels. A brand new canoe wore its glistening green canvas like a young woman in a new dress. Another was almost finished, the unpainted canvas stretched over it "like icing on a wedding cake," my husband said. He's not given to flights of fancy, but it did look just like creamy marzipan.

We indicated the ailing craft tied to the car. Is there any hope? Jim asked.

There was good news. The canoe could be fixed for less than the cost of buying a new one. Of course, we would have fixed it no matter what the cost. We had this canoe out on the big swells of Georgian Bay, in front of a wind so strong we stopped paddling and rigged up a towel for a sail.

John, the Canoe Company owner, was interested in the yoke. Had it come with the canoe? It's a replacement, we explained, for the one that broke when Jim was carrying the canoe down a railway line after the water on the Yamaska River ran out (we were living in Quebec then) and we had to walk home. The portage was going nicely until Jim stumbled and the canoe bounced up and came down hard. I've never understood why (but am grateful) it was the yoke that broke and not his shoulder.

We told John about paddling a couple of days to Maple Mountain. We found it swathed in fog, with rain pouring off the steep rocks that form the uppermost part of the trail. We decided to try for the top another day. He agreed with our wise choice. You could break a leg up there.

Our canoe will be ready soon. It'll have fresh green paint and it won't leak anymore. Jim and I have begun to plot our summer; which lakes are easily reached in a day's paddle, and which require a tent and a week's supply of bacon and coffee.

Perhaps we'll paddle in to Maple Mountain. We're pretty sure that this time we can make it to the top.

MAY 19 ❧ REGRET

For several days in 1990 I was one of the reporters at Oka, the 72-day standoff between Mohawk and authorities. It was a time of high tension, a fierce moment of confrontation between opposing values – on the one hand, a pine forest held in common; and on the other, a lucrative golf course.

I feel this fierce pang of regret whenever I think of the way land held in common – First Nations land, or public parks, or watersheds or forests – is still occasion for tension. Did I not tell the story well enough? But I did tell it, including the very beginning, the spiritual elder kindling a sacred fire on the road to the pines, offering prayers for bugs and birds and threatened trees.

The morning raid on that little campfire was an attack on a way of seeing the world. Perhaps my regret is that we still do not see the world that way and the assault continues. Perhaps

I should have tried harder, found ways to convert those whose values hurt the earth.

But the aboriginal and non-aboriginal people of the Americas and Australia have been living together for more than five hundred years now. Maybe there is more convergence of values than we think. Canadian author John Ralston Saul, for example, argues persuasively in *A Fair Country* that his country has been deeply influenced by aboriginal ideas, creating a balance between individualism and group interest that seems more First Nations than European.

I am proud of Canada's public institutions. I hope he is right.

Perhaps it is time to give up regret. Sometimes as a mother, I think that I have failed my children. There are many ways I could have been better. But that would fail to acknowledge the strength and power they have in abundance.

Sometimes as a citizen, I despair for our country. But that would fail to celebrate the strength of what we already are.

MAY 20 ❧ CHILDREN

Never imagine that children do not remember their childhood. Our children often describe things we said or did when they were very little. They do this with a mixture of affection and resolve, as if they had been saving up all these years to let us know how they felt.

Andy likes to play on my guilty-mother heart strings by describing his discomfort when we sent him, a shy, unilingual Anglophone, to a totally French-speaking kindergarten. He did not understand the language and when the teacher asked him if Santa Claus came at Christmas or Easter, he thought she was suggesting he climb under his desk, which he did.

Apparently the laughter of his classmates was quite traumatic.

This always elicits an apology from me, and a matching admission from him that it is now very good to be bilingual, even though it was hard then.

It is never too late for elders to explain their actions to their children.

MAY 21 ❧ BEAUTY

The maple is dropping tiny red blooms on the deck and the tulips are opening too fast. The shady side yard is a sea of white trilliums and I panic slightly whenever I walk through it. (Do not pick the provincial flower. Big fine. Maybe jail or beheading, every Ontario child learns this in school.) The forget-me-nots are a blue haze.

The yard is littered with pots and rakes and bicycles – the contents of the shed, which is getting new walls – and I am trying to hide the mess because this yellow mist of daffodils and leopard's bane and marsh marigolds lasts only for one minute, and then the meadow-rue and shasta daisies will be out instead and I will have missed the sweet woodruff, missed it completely.

I cannot keep up with all this beauty.

Indoors (as temporarily as possible), I note in a detached way dust balls on the stairs. No one has vacuumed for a month. Little clumps of mud have dried on the kitchen floor; I am too driven to care that I am infusing the garden into the house whenever I step inside.

It is spring in the north, the blurry hundred-shades-of-green month of May before the black flies and mosquitoes come to tell us how we pay for Eden. No matter. Charge what you like for paradise, I say to God who made all this. Only slow down time.

MAY 22 ❧ AFTER RETIREMENT

It is important to be bored sometimes, especially after a lifetime of strenuous work.

Probably this will be an unfamiliar sensation: wondering what to do with yourself, feeling restless and uneasy.

But there will be no real creativity ahead without these edgy moments. Go ahead, pace the floor, talk to yourself. Read. Wait. Weed a bit, if possible. Make soup, big pots of it, and store it in the freezer.

You will need soup when your vocation is revealed to you and you have no time to cook.

MAY 23 ❧ WARMING THE TOWELS

Huh. My grandson likes his after-bath towel warmed in the dryer. He loves to be bundled up in soft, hot terry, carried to the bedroom like a burrito, and dressed in warm pyjamas. Huh! Or should I say humbug. What a waste of energy. The whole planet is going to fall apart over this.

But what an act of love. And how delicious to be cuddled like this at the end of the day. And don't I wish that when I am old and frail and always cold, someone will warm my blanket and hold me with love?

Some days I am way too serious, and it gives conservation a bad name.

MAY 24 ❧ C. DIFFICILE

Amazing what you find out if you read indiscriminately. I didn't know that *Clostridium difficile* – the extremely nasty little organism we all rightly fear getting if we go into hospital and are treated with antibiotics – actually lives in some human stomachs quite harmlessly. It only gets to be a problem when antibiotics wipe out the other bacteria that live there and it grows without competition.

It's like many other invasive species. They do well because they are uniquely adapted to take advantage of certain conditions that humans create as we go about making life better. But perhaps the kudzu vine and zebra mussels and purple loosestrife are God's way of ensuring that life in some form will go on. A new ecology will sort itself out and find balance, and even pollution and clear-cutting and heavy metals in the water won't stop the exuberance of Creation.

I would prefer that humans be one of the favoured species.

MAY 25 ❧ THE VEGETABLE GARDEN

When I was a child growing up in a small northern village, we all had huge vegetable gardens. Was it the soil of Ontario's lesser clay belt, or the rural ethos, or simply post-World War II thrift? Whatever the reason, I am powerfully influenced by that example. I loved the inventiveness of those gardens and my dad's three compost piles, all the lawn cuttings and garden trash laced with manure and aged properly.

And he was raising me, talking to me – a very young girl – about what a good life and useful work were, even while the compost cooked and the perennials were transplanted and the raspberry canes were pruned so they didn't become a jungle.

All of this was mixed together at once, a recipe for life.

MAY 26 ❧ APPLE BLOSSOMS

Our old apple tree is growing next to the new tree, which is now almost as big as its elder. It still rains petals in a blizzard of youthful bloom each spring, and I stand beneath it, sometimes with Eli in my arms, and marvel at this springtime blizzard.

Apples are a symbol of immortality. The Greek goddess Hera was always pictured with the serpent guarding the apple-laden tree of life. Impelled by the human thirst for knowledge, Eve gave one to Adam. Later Avalon, apple-land, was the paradise to which King Arthur was carried when he died.

Small wonder one of Eli's first words was apple-*pomme*. The second August after his birth we held him so that he could grab the fruit of this ancient tree, held him up instinctively so that he could touch the wealth of ages.

MAY 27 ❧ TIKKUN OLAM

When Eli says grace he asks us to hold our hands around the table. Sometimes he just giggles, and someone else has to say it. Sometimes he simply states that for which he is grateful: "Thanks God for family." Or he begins with a long "ooooohh," a prelude to singing thankfully about apple seeds and rain.

This is the way we restore the world – constant prayer, prayer over every little thing. Orthodox rabbis and Celts know this. Every daily action is accompanied by prayer, a call for a blessing.

This day I seed the fields, set the table, churn the butter, bless the children.

We don't churn butter anymore. But we still say grace in our family, even – or maybe especially – when family is just my husband and me. It is good to bless the food of our tattered, warming, storm-tossed world.

MAY 28 ⁊ POTAGERIE

The thing about a garden is that it is one long and wonderful experiment for the future, at the same time as it remembers how things once were.

So I am experimenting with a *potagerie*, a mix of vegetables and flowers in one glorious confusion, just to see if it works and what it looks like. And it makes me nostalgic. It is like my father's garden. He grew frothy asparagus in the flower garden. I would cut the green ferns, though not all of them, for bouquets, and we ate the slender spears in early spring.

It is like the English cottage gardens, the small, densely planted plots labourers cultivated around their cottages. They had to keep some chickens and maybe a pig as well, so of course these gardens were never as romantic as the gardens that designers created later, in imitation.

I would like to keep chickens. Maybe a pig. It would be a wonderful experiment.

MAY 29 ✤ TRANSFORMATION

The subtle but powerful influence by First Nations United Church members became clear to me over the space of many General Councils, the triennial gatherings where our church as a national body determines its direction. At every Council, there would be a moment when the intervention of a Native elder would suddenly shift the whole 360-person assembly.

At one meeting I remember earth-shattering debate with long lines at the microphones, tears, passionate speeches, anger, doleful predictions. And then one of the commissioners, a Cree elder, got to his feet. The translator explained that his elder wished to pray. So the arena full of people silently bowed their heads, and the commissioner from a small community in northern Manitoba spoke for about 15 minutes. In Cree. Except for one English phrase which was scattered through his prayer. "Brothers and sisters," he said, and then continued in Cree. "Brothers and sisters." After several repetitions of these three words, the other 359 commissioners and youth and stewards and supportive staff – in fact, all the people who come together to act for the Church – remembered who they were. Brothers and sisters. Children of God. The deadlock was shattered and they addressed one another with respect.

The circle is always being repaired.

MAY 30 ❧ HOW TO SAVE THE WORLD

If we have an expansive front lawn, the first thing we could do to save the world is dig it up. Then plant a garden. There are many reasons for doing this. First, it creates abundant beauty, which reminds people that the earth is worth saving.

Second, a front garden makes a neighbourhood. People stop to admire the poppies and then they wonder how did you grow them? and when were they planted? and was it from seed? and could they have cuttings? and pretty soon they have been there all morning and you are having coffee together in the back yard. (But you should see the *back* yard.)

Third, quite often the front yard is where the sun is. In an old house like mine the back yard has become overgrown with shade trees and I cannot bear to cut them down. Once at a gardening talk, a woman asked me what she should do about her huge shade trees when she wanted to grow vegetables. We stared at each other in silence, because we both knew the truth. No matter how much she wanted that garden, she was not going to be able to sacrifice those trees.

The earth is saved by people acting together. So the first thing we do is dig up our front lawns and plant gardens.

MAY 31 ❧ CHANGING THE INTERPRETATION

Children, says author Isolina Ricci, are excellent observers but not good interpreters. So we go on into our adult lives basing our actions and moods on the faulty interpretation of the world we made when we were five.

This is why grandparents are important. We can watch for skewed interpretations and try to fix them: YES, you are loved. Or the next day, NO, this is not a sign that everyone is angry with you.

I hope that our grandson always notes accurately, and remembers, the uncontrollable and unconditional love he gets from Baba and me.

JUNE 1 ❧ WHAT DOES GOD LOOK LIKE?

Eli asks sometimes what God looks like. It's a bit complicated talking to four-year-olds about metaphors. I can't go wrong acquainting him with the Torah, I thought, so I have mentioned that God appeared to Moses as both a cloudy pillar and a burning bush.

I think I might try explaining that God is not very seeable, but we can see the actions of God as Nana's garden explodes with heavy pink peonies and oriental poppies and Siberian iris. (Maybe I won't use "explode.")

And then I will talk about the work of the bees, and the wind, and the rain, and the sun. Photosynthesis is a big word, but he is a smart boy. God's work, God's garden, and God is so kind as to allow us to pretend that, by moving plants and spreading around Jim's wonderful compost, it is "our" garden.

Eli may decide that God looks like a peony. And maybe he is right.

JUNE 2 ❧ GUERILLA GARDENERS

When my own garden is completely seeded – the nasturtium seeds tucked in about a half-inch deep, the Shirley and Icelandic poppies scattered as evenly and loosely as possible (no matter, they are going to come up crowded no matter what I do and I will have to thin them, wincing), the perennials that

I didn't divide last fall taken apart and replanted, and the pots (oh yes, the pots, I am afraid to count them) all planted up with surplus perennials and some annuals I just could not resist – my thoughts turn to other gardens.

Potential gardens. Guerrilla gardens. Gardens planted in the middle of the night on public land and in vacant lots. Vines covering ugly fences and boulevards overtaken with exuberance and colour.

I don't plant them all – who could – but in my mind's eye I have the plans. This fence could be completely covered with Virginia creeper. That blank and ugly wall, if it were covered with vines or espalier, would not then be available for graffiti artists. Why not give them another wall, of their own, and demand skill, not just tagging?

Long live those whose subversion assists Mother Earth, whose work slows runoff and casts shade and gobbles carbon, feeds the birds, and pleases the eye. Long live those who serve beauty.

JUNE 3 ❧ FOOD OF THE GODS

It was the first canoe trip of the summer. After a lot of paddling and portaging, Jim and I found a deserted, tree-covered, remote island on which to spend the night. We hauled up our canoe and set up our tent. When we began to move in our gear, we found that the tent smelled horribly of mildew.

Fortunately the weather was perfect. There were no flies. We threw our sleeping bags and camping mats on the ground and spent the night under the stars. For us, who are most of the time city-bound, the night sky was indescribably splendid.

The next morning, we rolled out of our sleeping bags, which were losing down stuffing rapidly and, like the tent, sadly in need of replacement. We expressed our gratitude that the weather was clear and warm and dry. We embarked on the best of all possible meals: bacon and eggs and toast and bush coffee over an open fire.

The wind came up. We had camped on a large rock outcrop with no way to peg our smelly tent to the ground. We turned from ecstatic contemplation of our coffee to see the tent lifting, then rolling like a giant tumbleweed across our tiny island. It sailed over the water for a bit, hit the surface, and slowly began to sink.

We laughed uncontrollably, on and on, despite our certain knowledge that if it began to rain we were without shelter. Finally Jim raced to the canoe and rescued the dead tent, not in order to use it again, but to avoid leaving garbage in the water.

It was the best canoe trip we ever had. We had transgressed the unbreakable rule (check your equipment carefully before you start out) and survived. The gods of the wilderness had smiled at our foolishness instead of taking retribution for our hubris; indeed, they had rewarded us with a sky full of diamonds.

The world is not always fair or just.

But we should note that sometimes that works to our benefit.

JUNE 4 ❧ BUSH COFFEE

Although I have offered this recipe in a previous book, I am including it here. When I worried about repeating myself in print, a good friend and former editor told me severely that nobody would remember what I had written some years before. (WHAT!) Making coffee in the bush is a skill everyone should have before they die.

Build a fire.

Set a pot of water in it.

When it is at a rolling boil, throw in quite a bit of ground coffee.

Boil for a few minutes.

Remove from fire. Let sit until the grounds sink to the bottom of the pot.

Pour.

You may need to repeat from step two. Go ahead. Do that. Make more toast, too, if you like. Do you have any idea how many calories are used in a day's hard paddle? You will have the strength of a god.

Hubris alert: Don't remark on that out loud.

JUNE 5 ❧ AMBITION

I am pursued by demons
do more do more
be admired

Swish swash
back and forth
their brisk claws push me
to and fro.

Their harsh sounds compel my dreams:
"Accomplish"
"Win"

And never mind, no mind for the garden
The moment of blossom
The rain
The soft dark, the tender soil and worms.

That's for later, they whisper, later. Later.

JUNE 6 ❧ GUILT

I need to take some days off from visiting my mother in her nursing home, following her stay in the emergency ward at the hospital. I think I can take that time now. Of course it will make her angrier than ever. She does rage. But I will have to leave her to it for a few days.

Survivor guilt. I could write a treatise about it, how it wakes me up at 3:00 a.m. wondering if I remembered to phone her, wondering where they have moved those damned medical socks in the store, wondering if I have signed every paper and paid every bill, and what will we do if her money runs out?

Guilt is useless and tiring. No one else can rest me. I must rest myself.

JUNE 7 ❧ DEER TICKS AND WEST NILE VIRUS

It's easy to be afraid of nature, I think, as I tuck my jeans into my socks preparatory to a hike in the woods. (How big is a deer tick? How do I know if I have Lyme's disease?) I don rubber gloves to pick up a dead blue jay beneath my window. (Did it hit the glass, or succumb to West Nile virus?)

To be human is to be anxious, cautious, careful. I believe in this. That's why I send my children off with the mantra "drive safely," as if this will somehow prevent pile-ups on the highway.

But we can't let it destroy our ability to go out into the natural world. If we are not in it, we will not love it. If we do not love it, we will allow it to shrink and disappear.

JUNE 8 ❧ WOMAN ELDER

Rita O'Sullivan was the second chief of the Teme-Augama Anishnabai when she attended a large meeting held at one of our local churches. It became harshly confrontational. Rita stood up, went to the microphone, and simply waited there, tall, white-haired, dignified. The silence stretched.

After everything was very calm, Rita began to talk, gently out-lining the piece of history of her First Nation that was relevant to the discussion. People listened carefully. The heat seemed to dis-sipate, leaving only attention and compassion in the room.

Rita sat down and the meeting continued, graciously.

That is an elder's presence.

JUNE 9 ❧ MY MOTHER

My mother had a visit from Andy, her second-oldest grand-son. "What would you like to do, Grandma?" he asked. "Would you like to go for a walk?"

Some time before, she had made the move, unwillingly, from an assisted-living residence to a full-scale nursing home that could provide constant support. It was becoming harder and harder for her to walk or even feed herself. A wheelchair was now a full-time presence in her room. But she wanted to go back for a visit to her former residence, located not so far away if you were able-bodied.

So Andy helped her into her coat and her chair, and they set off. The sidewalk was bumpy for a wheelchair, but Grandma wanted to persist. The sun was bright, so she wore Andy's sun visor, an odd but appealing accessory to her trench coat and wheelchair.

Bump, bump, bump. This probably wasn't comfortable for Grandma's increasingly frail spine, but on they went.

When they arrived, there was nobody there that she knew. Her favourite staff person was off-duty, and the residents she counted as her friends had dispersed to nursing homes or died. Old age can be cruel.

They bumped back to her nursing home. But despite their lonely reception and her uncomfortable ride, my mother was blissful. For an entire hour, her grandson had paid attention to her alone. They had a glass of sherry together afterwards. (Andy hates sherry, but Grandma won't drink by herself. In any case, her total blindness means that she can't see that his glass is entirely fictitious.)

Happiness in our frail old age is defined not by comfort, but by love.

JUNE 10 ❧ A PLAN

We need to have vocational counselling for elders.

As a young woman, it was stupendously helpful to have personality tests and aptitude tests and interviews and conversations about what the experts had found out about me. Just the sort of thing I love. It gave me renewed confidence that I could embark consciously on the career I had fallen into – writing – and survive.

It would be good for elders to have a similar plan, a set of goals, for the rest of their lives.

My first goal would be to keep in touch with the natural world. We worry about children today who lack wild places to play. We should also worry about elders who lack a place to put their hands in the soil, or a meadow to walk in instead of on pavement.

I am going to keep agitating for parks. Also, I am considering how to start a war on asphalt.

JUNE 11 ❧ A PLAN TWO

I have a second goal for my good life as an old elder. I will refuse to be separated from life by a glowing screen of any size or description. It must be tempting to spend one's very old eldership in front of the television, just as it is tempting now to relate to the universe through my computer.

My plan to equip myself for life later, is to have so many good friends of such variety that some of us will be left to talk to one another, and go for slow walks together, leaving the glowing screens behind.

JUNE 12 ❧ A PLAN THREE

Beauty keeps us attached to the earth. Whatever I hear about life hereafter – golden streets or cosmic dust, reincarnation or oblivion – I don't hear much discussion about the way sunlight splashes over my humble pole beans, or the angular lines of a granite outcrop beneath a big pine.

Popular conceptions of heaven involve a lot of fluffy clouds. Nobody takes this seriously except, apparently, television ad producers. Still, heaven as an energetic city bursting with discussion over coffee and imaginative city squares and trees, trees, trees doesn't figure in anyone's future projections as far as I know.

So I propose elders guard beauty here on earth, and stick around to enjoy it as long as we can. We could befriend a sympathetic architect or civic designer for advice, and appear on beauty's behalf whenever new developments are proposed. We could discuss proportion and context, scale and imagination, pedestrian traffic, birdsong, and trees. Elders could speak for beauty.

JUNE 13 ❧ POLITICAL ELDER

My friend Alice, about my age, called in the middle of an election campaign. She had called the day before and I had agreed to put a sign on our front lawn. It's an easy path to virtue, and I admire our local candidate.

The next night she called me again, wondering if I would take a sign for our front lawn. "But you called me last night," I said.

She apologized. She had mixed up the phone list. We chatted. She apologized again, saying that she was making 70 phone calls a day and it was easy to get confused.

Seventy phone calls a day.

That is passionate engagement. Engagement keeps elders alive. Alice is going to live forever.

JUNE 14 ❧ HOUSE SHOPPING

About once every three years or so, we go house shopping, which is strange, because we love our house dearly.

But there's a bit of an "if not now, when?" quality to being an elder, a desire to live with what really matters to us. So we are looking at houses in the bush, with wood stoves. It is ridiculous for two people with a combined age of about 140 years to be considering heating and cooking with wood, carrying big chunks of it in, and ashes out.

We must be crazy. But water matters to us, trees matter to us, and we would be surrounded by both. At the same time, we would be far from doctors' and dentists' offices, far from grocery stores and libraries.

We can walk to the library now. Really, this makes no sense.

But to be an elder is to know that the time is short, and dreams let go will not return.

JUNE 15 ❧ LEFT BEHIND

We do a lot of digging in June. It's a gentle time, with long sunny days. Dividing perennials and augmenting borders makes you strong.

So it's not a bad time for elders to look back over our lives and see what aspects of our character we have buried. Maybe it is time to dig them up and make them part of ourselves. Reaching towards wholeness is what life is about. And our lives are getting shorter.

Perhaps I buried a kind of softness of heart. Working as a journalist, I could not afford to be undone by tragedy. In El Salvador, I spent one noon hour listening to a young woman describe her torture at the hands of government thugs. I took notes and taped while the non-writers around me listened with tears pouring down their cheeks. If I was going to tell her story, I needed to write it down. I could not afford blurry pages.

Working as a writer out of my own home, I could not afford to be sidetracked by needy people. I limited invitations for lunch and coffee, shortened phone conversations. The invention of call display was a godsend.

But now I have to look at what was dredged out of my life. Perhaps I ripped away too much. Now I am undone by any difficulty faced by one I love. I am no longer able to shunt pain into a different compartment and carry on.

Now I am more whole.

JUNE 16 ⚘ HIKING

Young Mowat, who is four, and Maese, almost three, and their mom – our daughter's friends – took us hiking on Quadra Island in British Columbia. We climbed and climbed. At the top of Chinese Mountain, Mowat clambered onto a big rock and offered an impromptu concert. "All I really need," he sang, "is food in my belly and love in my family." Or words to that effect.

Maese climbed up next. "Don't go near the edge," she sang, in the manner of a mountain-proofed child. "Don't go near the edge."

There were edges all around, and love too, and food in our bellies, and our daughter and her friends.

It is all we really need.

JUNE 17 ⚘ DREAMS OF SMOKE

I dreamed I was in the neighbourhood walking up the street. They were building a new house, two doors from our own. There was a big vegetable garden in between. Jim came out of our house. I asked what would be the consequence of the new house. Noise? If it burned, there would be toxic smoke.

It did burn. We had to flee to my mother's house.

For psychoanalyst Carl Jung, the writings of 19th-century alchemists provided a treasury of symbol and theory that remains valuable to dreamers. The alchemists were concerned with transforming base metals into gold, just as our dreams are concerned with our personal transformation.

Nothing transforms like fire.

So I don't think this dream is bad news. The things I love are here – neighbourhood, vegetable gardens, Jim, home, my mother. Clearly I am weighing the consequence of change and the anger ("toxic smoke") this entails. Change often brings anger, which doesn't mean we can't ever change, just that we need to be ready to work it through.

Even for an elder, life is full of necessary change. Watch for dreams of fire, and don't be alarmed. Just brace yourself.

JUNE 18 ⚘ ELDERS AND ELDERS

I know that my mother was an elder. Indeed, she was a wise woman – for others. For me she was cranky and vulnerable and only sometimes kind.

This might mean that your own parent cannot be your elder. Or it might mean that this particular elder knows the truths that are very hard for you to bear, and that are therefore most valuable.

JUNE 19 ❧ BANNERS

We went to the train station to wish our friend Priscilla Solomon well. There was a little crowd of people there, some carrying beautiful hand-made banners. Priscilla was taking them to Ottawa as part of a cross-country effort to persuade our government to implement the United Nations Declaration of Indigenous Rights, signed several months before.

Priscilla is Ojibway, the daughter of Art and Eva Solomon, both highly respected elders in their lifetimes. She is a nun, a sister of Saint Joseph. Our friend Elizabeth gave her a small pouch of tobacco and offered a prayer. We stood in the heat and prayed for justice for aboriginal people and then Priscilla, smiling, packed up the banners and took them with her on the train.

After she came back, we ran into her on the street. She told us that there had been so many vivid banners from all over Canada that, joined together, they stretched up and down Wellington Street in front of the Parliament Buildings for over a kilometre. They were carried to the beat of drums, and raised up by hundreds of willing hands. There was laughter. There were speeches and songs and dances by elders and young people, First Nations and not.

I didn't see anything about this in the newspapers or on the television news. But Priscilla is not downhearted. Elders persist with joy.

JUNE 20 ❧ SUMMER SOLSTICE

Bless the large gray owl who sits immobile glaring down at me.
Bless the conscientious robin catching worms.
Bless the smart crow tearing into garbage making mess.
Bless the mourning dove, her sadness.
Bless the hummingbird, returned at last.
Bless the angels.
Amen.

JUNE 21 ❧ QUESTION ONE FOR AN ACTIVIST ELDER

It was a several-day-long workshop on forest management. I was writing a cover article on the fate of the boreal forest, and the experts speaking here offered valuable background to a story I wanted fiercely.

One elderly couple kept popping up to the microphone. They demanded attention. I found myself increasingly annoyed, even though their critique of the experts' data matched my own. They were against vast clear-cuts, and for diverse usage of the forest; hunting mushrooms and picking blueberries, they felt, were important uses for the valuable land. They were right. And in their very rightness and persistence and sheer unmitigated contrariness, they were also annoying.

Hence a question for an activist elder: Am I predictable to the point of annoyance?

JUNE 22 ❧ QUESTION TWO FOR AN ACTIVIST ELDER

The same woman is always at the microphone. She was there at last year's annual meeting as well. She is saying all the right things. She does her research and she knows a great deal about injustice in all parts of the world. She looks awfully tired, and I have not seen her smile once in the three days that I have been here. Her work is bringing her no joy, even though it is very, very worthy work. She needs, I thought, a sabbatical.

Another question for an activist elder: Am I continuing on a set path that excludes a life task I need to do?

JUNE 23 ❧ QUESTION THREE FOR AN ACTIVIST ELDER

Once I dreamed of a Nazi climbing to a tower with a machine gun, and shooting everything around.

My dreams generally tell me if I have become disrespectful to those I am attempting to persuade. It is so easy, when you are fighting for social justice, to be taken over by the issue at hand. Deaf ears call for louder and louder shouting. Why can't they hear me?

A third question for an activist elder: Are your dreams full of interesting puns that hint in their lopsided dream fashion that you are not doing this respectfully? Watch for weapons (shooting people down) and smoke (righteous, but choking, anger).

JUNE 24 ❧ QUESTION FOUR FOR AN ACTIVIST ELDER

I had been covering the actions of a group of nuns and other religious women. We were just back from Honduras, where they had tried to draw the world's attention to American dealings with the dictatorship in power. Concerned that this tiny impoverished country was allowing a military airstrip and hospital to be built preparatory to an American invasion of equally impoverished Nicaragua next door, the sisters had embarked on a "pilgrimage to the place of evil" to pray.

Our plane landed in Honduras twice, but each time armed soldiers turned us back, so we went instead to Washington. The sisters' connections found us all a place at a Jesuit school. There were no beds, but no problem. We had come prepared to camp out on a runway.

Exhausted, I found a place on the carpeted floor of the library, unrolled my sleeping bag, and slid in. My toes encountered a peculiar lump. I reached down and pulled out a familiar red and blue figure. My daughter's soft stuffed Smurf had accompanied me to Honduras, the encounters with the military, and a Congressional press conference.

Tracy was five, and her mother had been unreasonably preoccupied for days. She had inserted it into my sleeping bag before I left, to keep me safe or to remind me of her, I don't know.

It raises another question for the activist elder: Are you neglecting anyone you love in your quest for justice?

JUNE 25 ❧ QUESTION FIVE FOR AN ACTIVIST ELDER

We were in the middle of a fight to save a park. Citizens were incensed, packing the council chambers and making the kind of heartfelt presentations that can only be made by someone who loves a piece of common land and knows what a neighbourhood needs to be healthy.

Some of our group had met the night before. Now, as their spokesperson, I was ready to make yet another impassioned speech on behalf of this piece of land. But as others spoke first, I could hear our carefully-thought-out points echoing around the chambers. We had the tenth speaking slot. By then everything we wanted to say about the importance of parks in this area had been said. I went to the microphone and said that GreenSpace would not be using its allotted time because all of our points had been covered. I summarized the previous speakers' rationale briefly, said we agreed, and sat down.

Councillors, used to hearing me hold forth, looked startled.

My fellow GreenSpacers had mixed reactions. Some agreed, others felt that we should never have given up the chance to drive a point home. I didn't sleep that night. Had I let the side down? Especially after several busy people had given up an evening to help me frame the points?

I still don't know if that was the right thing to do. I will never know. But I think it is a question activist elders need to ask themselves: Am I speaking because I like the sound of my own voice, or because this is something new and informative for the audience?

JUNE 26 ❧ QUESTION ONE FOR A NON-ACTIVIST ELDER

For some of us, it is very hard to protest when something is wrong. I prefer to garden. Or hide under the bed. It is desperately hard for some to hold up a placard, or sign our names to an angry letter, or stand up and read a statement in public.

But when children are hungry in one of the wealthiest countries on earth, it does raise a difficult question: Am I using the experience of my years to speak out about what's wrong?

JUNE 27 ❧ QUESTION TWO FOR A NON-ACTIVIST ELDER

The opposite of fear is not courage. Courage and fear nearly always go hand in hand. People do not stand up to the powerful, or risk looking undignified in public because they are fearless. They do so because living with the pain of injustice – for themselves or others – is more powerful than their fear.

If I do not yet have the courage to speak out, when?

JUNE 28 ❧ QUESTION THREE FOR A NON-ACTIVIST ELDER

I am a master at figuring out how whatever I have to do each day is very important. Crucial. I can make myself much too busy doing these things to make time to oppose bad behaviour in governments at any level. And watching the parliamentary channel must raise my blood pressure. I am sure of that. Too much stress (in the form of watching the daily news) is bad for my health. I am sure of that too.

But. Am I doing what I can to leave a healthy world for everybody's grandchildren?

This question requires qualifying, of course. I know a multitude of women who do far more than I do to make a healthy world. Without any apparent fatigue, they make home-cooked meals for those without homes, wash dishes and bake cookies, and weed, and plant trees. We don't always have to make noise to make things better.

JUNE 29 ❧ QUESTION FOUR FOR A NON-ACTIVIST ELDER

Elders should expect respect from others. They have the knowledge that comes with a long life, and they have survived whatever life has thrown at them. Life throws something hard at every person.

Elders also need to model respect for others. It is quite possible that you, as an elder, know how to disagree with others in a gracious way, simply differentiating yourself from their policies. You give them room to think differently, but ultimately make it clear where you stand, and how the consequences of their actions will be harmful.

If you know how to do this, why not speak out and show others how to do so as well?

JUNE 30 ❧ THE TIME BEFORE

When they go I will exhale.

For now I hold my breath.
Four days left to hold this small body and
Watch small fingers prowl through Nana's cupboards and
Whisper hush hush at night and
Walk to Twigg's for lunch (but he falls asleep half-way).

Breathe breathe, but I cannot.

When he comes back he will be bigger. Perhaps there will be no snow and we will play baseball, and Eli and Baba will camp out in the back yard and
We will go to the beach and throw stones across the water, skip skip skip.

But in between, how will we breathe, Baba and me?

JULY 1 ❧ OLD THINGS

I have always loved old things. Old pine furniture and old growth forests (yes, those two *are* contradictory), old houses and churches and post offices and railway stations. So my husband's white hair – which he notes with a degree of ambivalence – similarly fills me with delight.

It's a mark of our culture's asymmetry, though, that old people are not generally held in such high regard as old things. A long time ago, a close-up of an elderly woman's face appeared on the cover of the magazine where I worked. It was a warm and beautiful portrait, but it included age spots and double chin. Some readers wrote in to complain, and the subject was herself a little ambivalent over her photo.

Children handle aging much better, which may be why we all love grandchildren so much. "How long does it take," Eli asked one day, "from child to wrinkly?" He didn't seem concerned, although he was gazing intently at my face. He was just interested.

Old age is indeed interesting. And "old" is not a swear word. But maybe we should do with it as Meg Hickling, sex educator, suggests we do with sex-linked body parts: run the vacuum and shout the words into the noise until we can say them without flinching. "Penis." "Vagina." "Old." "Old." "OLD!"

JULY 2 ❧ LILIES

Consider the lilies of the field, how they grow; they neither toil nor spin,
yet I tell you even Solomon in all his glory was not arrayed like one of
these..." Jesus (Matthew 6:28, 29 – English Standard Version)

Lilies are on my mind. My garden would have none if I did
not go out early every morning to grab and squash violently
all the little red lily beetles before they munch up the garden's
most gorgeous flowers.

Most satisfying things do involve effort. There is an intense
creative joy in much of what we call "work." If I were to lie in the
hammock all day, I would miss the rush.

I think Jesus merely suggests here that we refrain from despair when we face a daunting task. We are always caught between twin forces: anxiety, which propels us to action; and trust,
which gives us courage. He is encouraging us to trust in God
and in our own aggressive energy.

In Judaism, that energy has a name. It is called the *yetzer hara*.
It is the yearning, the desire, the lust for all that is vital to life.
It is like the illogical courage of two-and-a-half-ounce robins
warning off immense humans. It is best mingled with *yetzer tov*,
the impulse towards goodness.

Yetzer hara must be controlled, but not destroyed. Without, I
could not crush the lily beetles.

JULY 3 ❧ ELI'S GRACE

Eli's grace is sometimes, "Everyone is here." Other times it consists of showing us how to fold our hands, as they do at daycare, and saying, "And God thanks us for His food."

It makes me wonder. Perhaps Eli knows something. Perhaps God is grateful to us, and regards us as colleagues and companions in God's great order of Creation. Not often, given our penchant for polluting it. But when we are dumbstruck by beauty, perhaps God heaves a sigh of relief and says, "Thanks for noticing that." When we do something especially clever, like learning how to grow peaches, or wheat, perhaps God says, "Oh, good on you," just the way my Australian friend does, and which makes me feel terrific.

Does God need us? Would Creation be any fun without God's recalcitrant children who mostly get things wrong, so wrong, and who then once in a while look up amazed and say with a brilliant smile, "Everyone is here."

JULY 4 ❧ GRATITUDE

When my mother became ill for the last time, I began to understand more fully how siblings love one another. My brother and sister-in-law made the long trip to see her – five hours each way – frequently and without complaint. My brother phoned her often, listening patiently to her woes. I usually, grumpily, left the room when the litany became too severe.

The summer before my mother died my brother and sister-in-law built a deck for us, a way of marking the fact that I lived nearest to our mother and carried, of necessity, much of her care.

The fact that my brother has been totally blind for many years made no difference to this project. He told us what to buy, and each day my sister-in-law and I went to the lumber store and bought what was needed: this number of deck boards of this size, this many pounds of deck screws, this many cans of preservative. Although Jim usually did it, my brother also ran the power saw, cutting boards to the appropriate length. I went around unplugging the saw whenever possible, terrified he would damage himself, although he has been working this way most of his life.

When my brother had an idea for a huge planter as part of the deck, but thought we might have to postpone it for a few months, my sister-in-law insisted we finish it before they left. It took just under a week.

Our deck has two generous levels, angled towards the southwest corner of the big back yard. It is shaded by our beloved huge maple tree (which my brother took care to keep undamaged) and every summer the planter is filled with impatiens and tuberous begonia, perennial geranium, and lady's mantle.

Whenever I sit on it, I am reminded of my mother, cared for by her children who cared for each other. I am reminded of my sister-in-law, the sole driver making the long car trip uncom-

plainingly, year after year. I am reminded of my husband, happily and humbly and trustingly following the directions of his
brother-in-law who knows how to build things he can't see.

And I am grateful.

JULY 5 ❧ OATMEAL

M y Scottish grandmother made oatmeal for breakfast.
That might be why she lived to be 93, and also why I love
oatmeal.

Oatmeal has many virtues. It fills me up at breakfast, so that
I am not suddenly starving at 10:30 a.m., otherwise my habit.
It apparently lowers the bad kind of cholesterol, and does not
produce the insulin spike that creates my usual mid-morning
hunger. Oatmeal accepts blueberries or strawberries, almonds
or walnuts gracefully, along with a tiny bit of maple syrup and
some skim milk.

Of course, if you are thin and active, you can top it with butter and brown sugar and cream. I am not thin, but hope for this
takes my breath away.

Conversely – and again, this is just a rumour – a strict short-
term diet of oatmeal and water, later morphing into oatmeal and
fruit and water – causes rapid weight loss. That's if you stick to
half a cup per meal. I couldn't be so mingy with my beloved cereal, and anyway I disapprove of fad diets and trendy miracle foods.

But it is tempting.

If you are an elder with an ancestor from Scotland somewhere in your family tree, you could try eating oatmeal for breakfast. Your genes might recognize it. You might live to be 93.

JULY 6 ❧ PSYCHIC PAIN

Psychic pain (as opposed to physical pain) is often soothed by considering that tomorrow might be better. From experience, elder women know this. We remember that the tomorrows of other times have been better.

Going to a strange place, for example, is always difficult for an introvert like me. But over many years of necessary travel I learned that, after about 24 hours, the new place seems a little... familiar. I learned to trust my powers of adaptation and resilience. I learned to say to myself, "Remember. In about a day, I will get more used to this hotel/meeting/country/people. I will speak more freely with them. Things will be brighter."

So it is in these strange countries called pain and remorse. The emotional scar begins to heal, the catastrophe looks a little more bearable in daylight, time begins to work its magic. Soon we can speak to mend the rift.

Be wise about this. It may have been an entirely necessary conflict; the rift cannot be closed too soon. It may take much longer than 24 hours. But tomorrow will come, some day.

JULY 7 ✤ SISTER MARGARET

Sister Margaret Smith is one of my elder women. I watch her closely so as to learn from her how she uses the power of the elder. I got to know Sister Margaret through my husband, who is a minister. They are both people with a highly specific vocation, a religious calling, hence the honorifics "sister" and "reverend."

Their respect for one another is profound and beautiful. One is a Roman Catholic nun and retired hospital director; the other a minister and retired chief executive officer in a liberal Protestant denomination. It is highly likely that there are articles of faith upon which they disagree. But I believe they have in common a deep humanity that would simply drown any difference in doctrine.

They both once had power. They both now have influence, which is different. They both held highly responsible and demanding jobs in organizations – the two largest denominations in Canada, in fact – that have been undergoing intense change and public scrutiny. They both retained their faith.

I don't know how they did this exactly, but I watch and try to learn.

JULY 8 ✤ MANAGING POLITICIANS

Courage is important when attempting to influence politicians, especially if we feel they are headed in the wrong direction. I am not brave. But I did witness small Bible study groups at a *kirchentag* in East Berlin before the wall came down. The members talked openly about the importance of salt, which they interpreted as acts of defiance by Christians in a repressive society. The Stasi, the East German secret police, were present. These members of the study who talked this way were risking a prison term, or their children being barred from university, or both.

It makes the act of holding a placard in a protest march seem like nothing.

JULY 9 ❧ POTENTIAL

A minister friend says he used to listen to my husband in astonishment when they discussed the best way to deal with certain difficult individuals. Were they talking about the same person? Then he decided that Jim was addressing the *potential* within that person for good.

In Jewish theology, each human being carries within themselves the potential for both goodness and wickedness. That is what makes us humans. (Angels lack these passionate forces within.)

Both energies – for good and for evil – are important. We cannot survive without the wild energy that feeds our non-angelic passions: greed and lust and anger. We also need the other necessary human instinct, the one for good.

It might be a little boring to be an angel.

In any case we have no choice. We are human. We have to be what we are. But we can speak to the goodness in others, which we know is all the more valuable because it co-exists with the passion that gives us raging life.

JULY 10 ❧ THE DINING TABLE

Wherever it is, in Jewish theology the family dining table is holy. After the destruction of the Second Temple in Jerusalem in 70 BCE, the holiest place became "not the synagogue," says author Wendy Mogel, "but our own homes."

I agree. In our home, the dining table is where we talk to each other and to God. Grace, for many of us, is the one formal prayer we say all day. Here around the table – even when the meal is raucous and hurried, when teens might be sullen and rebellious, little ones might be eager and noisy, old ones might be cranky – is where we can count on an acknowledgement that God is among us.

When each of my children came into possession of a dining table, I breathed out a breath I hadn't known I was holding. One child gathers friends around a shiny square of polished glass, one around a circle of battered oak, and one around a tiny circle big enough for three. No matter. Friends gather, food is given, ideas and laughter surface.

Aaah! God is with them.

JULY 11 ❧ FITNESS

If elders don't stay in shape, they will be reminded to do so. I have a stiff neck. It started when I began to sit at the computer for long periods of time to write this book. Methodically, I go over the possible reasons for this: Is it a sign that I am being rigid (stiff-necked) about something? Is my body declaring that this book should not be written, that I am neglecting my spouse in our long-awaited retirement? Am I forgetting about keeping my aging body in shape?

Oops.

Now I get up from my desk every 20 minutes and do an idiosyncratic collection of exercises, hoping to make up for the fact that I have temporarily abandoned the gym and my wonderful trainer. A small internal voice had told me that (a) "You need uninterrupted days of work on the manuscript," and (b) "Saving money is good." There may be a (c) in there too: "Why are you spending money and time to have someone else keep you fit when you *should* be capable of doing it yourself?"

That voice was wrong. Everything I read in my daily paper, as well as the exhortations of my children, suggest the words "elder" and "fitness" need to be found in the same sentence.

Responsible elders offer advice, so I am doing so: Don't make my mistake. Don't abandon fitness on the counsel of a devilish internal voice.

JULY 12 ❧ PARADOX

From my journal at the time:

My mother is dying. Or so we believe. She was placed on palliative care a few weeks ago, unresponsive, sleeping, dying. I came into her room and found a brochure about what to expect as people begin to fade.

That was a few weeks ago. I have lost track. She has rallied and sunk, rallied and declined. Today so far is a rally day. I went in to give her breakfast, and she spoke, asking for her dry cereal (the staff doesn't like her to have it lest she choke, but she was firm. So we soaked her Rice Krispies in a lot of milk). When I gave her the second cup of coffee, after her yoghurt and banana, I absent-mindedly offered it to her (through a straw) while it was still too hot. I am afraid Bad Daughter is back, after all these days of tender care. Oops. She spewed it out and regarded me furiously. I felt terrible.

It did make me think she might decide not to die. I have come to believe that one of the reasons she has lived so long – into her 97th year – is that whenever she receives from me the always-on-call care she has coveted these twenty-five years, she changes her mind about dying. Also, my friends are coming in, and they are so tender with her. I would certainly decide to live too.

And there are overwhelmingly gentle moments with each distant grandchild. We hold the phone (set on speaker for added volume) to her ear. Each time, we hear – to our continuing astonishment – my mother choke out a full sentence: "I love you too."

JULY 13 ❧ THE LIGHT

For some 12th-century mystics like Hildegard of Bingen, God became simply light. Contemporary theologian Dorothee Soelle was drawn to this image because, she said, light is not powerful or violent. It does not command, or demand sacrifices. It just illumines the world. We simply immerse ourselves in it. The mystics immersed themselves in God.

I remember this on Sunday mornings as I drown in the light pouring through stained glass from four directions, a whole circle of light.

JULY 14 ❧ VACATION PHOTOS

The best vacation visit ever is over. Our grandson Eli protested his way into the car and – hours later – we received the call that they were safely home.

Now we are looking at masses of photos documenting picnics on the beach, daring feats at the playground, and water fights in the back yard.

We will circulate all these proudly until the relatives cry uncle.

But perhaps, I think to myself, perhaps not the photos with Nana in them. Because aging has invoked the immutable law of gravity. The evidence – captured digitally – is unavoidable. My whole face has floated downwards, including the corners of my mouth. I look serious in these photos, although in actual fact I was having a sensational time.

This happens to elders. Our facial structure no longer reflects our inner world. Perhaps this is what gives rise to the stereotypes of (a) cranky old people or (b) deep thinkers engrossed in saving humanity.

I consider my photos carefully. I find some in which I am laughing, a true reflection of my inner joy. But in these I seem to have an extra chin. No matter what I do, these pictures firmly confront me with the life-change known as old age.

So I turn to William Bridges, whose book *Transitions: Making Sense of Life's Changes* is the classic text for such confusing times. He explains how, earlier in life, the development of a "self-image and personal style" makes the important life-change from dependence to independence possible. But then – much later – comes a time when "that same self-image and style hinders growth, and the person must go through the long, slow process of growing beyond them."

For five glorious years I have been growing into being a Nana. The delights of story-reading and beach-exploring with grandchildren are accompanied by the physical changes those years bring. Few of us get to be young, firm-faced career women and muffin-baking grandmas at the same time.

Tomorrow, when the family opens up their emails, they will find a hundred shots of Eli and some of Nana too. Both of us are laughing.

JULY 15 ❧ LISTENING TO THE SERMON

This is the only time in the week when I listen to someone speak and cannot reply. Since it is not considered good form during a sermon to stand up and say, "Oh, that makes me think of...," or, "Well, have you considered...," I hear without comment, turning the ideas over in my mind.

I used to do this in my writing classes. We would go around the circle, each person reading aloud what they had written, the others simply listening. No comment allowed.

It means we have to let things settle in. It means we can't immediately bounce an idea back with our own spin on it. We have to be hospitable. We have to give the idea houseroom (even if we don't agree), and feed it, and give it a place to sleep.

Something happens when this occurs in a group, a kind of tenderness. The whole community begins to care gently for this idea. We sit on a Sunday morning, each one listening in our own way. Thoughts meander. We are not used to paying attention to one voice for 20 minutes in our culture. But since our thoughts have nowhere to meander except inside our own heads, they circle around and come back, renewed.

We are carried in this way by our tradition. What happens here is valuable. It is a little yeasting of ideas that ferments through the week, a little hosting within each person's psyche of an ancient sacred text brought forward through the centuries to our prideful, postmodern, deconstructed world. A little earnestness made welcome.

Elders know about this listening, and we are keeping it alive.

JULY 16 ❧ GARDEN TOURS

Sometimes we host the symphony garden tour. The orchestra sends a musician or two to play in the garden and an artist comes to work with clay or paint or a camera. Jim and I are very proud of our part in this.

Usually the weather in July is hot (although one summer it was so cold on tour day we had to wrap the ticket-sellers in Hudson's Bay blankets to keep them warm). But one year it rained. This is a disaster, I thought. The musician packed away his viola and the artist, a potter, couldn't set up her wheel. The skies teemed, and we thought that nobody would come.

And then, only a few minutes past the scheduled opening time, I looked out the window. The garden was a sea of bright, wet umbrellas. Children were racing from the shelter of one umbrella to another, laughing, while the adults – gardeners all – ignored the downpour and admired the intense colour of rain-soaked leaves and blossoms.

Over 300 people wandered through our back yard that day. Jim and I, dripping happily in our waterproof ponchos, answered questions about compost and tried to remember the name of every plant.

I had never before appreciated the solidarity between gardening humans and thirsty plants. But I do now.

JULY 17 ❧ ACCUMULATION

When the children were young we had a camp in the bush. Jim inherited the family rowboat, a beautiful cedar-strip antique, and the children and our guests spent hours piloting it around our tiny lake. Photos from the time show young boaters rowing madly, trying to create a speedboat effect for whoever was on the old inner tube they dragged behind.

One winter the rowboat was stolen from its hiding place under the cabin. The thieves left the oars, which had been safely stored indoors.

We acquired a hard lesson along with our broken hearts. We already had a canoe that we carried home on top of the car each summer. We couldn't carry the rowboat as well. Perhaps one should only accumulate what one can carefully look after.

The rowboat is gone (I hope whoever has it cares for it – these things need varnish fairly often) but our children remain to us: grownup, loving, and strong. Maybe that rowboat is part of their grown-up strength, inherited from those lazy summer days when they were set loose to explore a lake – whose entire length their parents could monitor – on their own.

JULY 18 ❧ SITTING IN THE BALCONY

When a suggestion was made to stop using our church balcony during worship, I found myself vociferously opposed. I like to sit up there. I like to look down on the congregation below and hold them in my heart. The ceiling of the sanctuary is old dark wood, constructed by ship-builders. When you are in the balcony you are close to its curves, as if you are carrying your canoe.

I like the little society that gathers in the balcony; a small group, but mighty. We each have our individual reasons for wanting to worship there, I am sure. But they must be strong reasons, because most of us up there are elders and we still trudge up those stairs.

I like the quiet. Ours is a very communal church, as church should be. We greet each other with delight, we tell each other about our week. I love that. But some days I go to church knowing that unshed but necessary tears are just below the surface, and the balcony is a little dark sanctuary where I can struggle through hymns sniffling into a tissue without worrying too many people too much.

Love and beauty and tears. People living life in all its rigour might need to know about the balcony. There is room up there.

JULY 19 ❧ POTLUCK RECIPE

The best potluck dish at this time of year is a huge salad. All the ingredients are fresh and inexpensive. But if it looks as if everyone is going that route you could try this easy and very old-fashioned dessert, which will add to your elder credentials.

1 cup flour
2 teaspoons baking powder
¾ cup sugar
2 tablespoons cocoa
½ cup milk
2 tablespoons butter, melted
1 cup chopped walnuts (optional if allergies are a concern)
1 cup brown sugar
¼ cup cocoa
1¾ cups hot water

Preheat oven to 350°F. Mix flour, baking powder, sugar, and 2 tablespoons cocoa in a bowl. Stir in the milk and butter. Blend in nuts. Spread in a greased 9-inch square pan, or a casserole dish of approximately that size. Mix the brown sugar and ¼ cup cocoa together and sprinkle on top. Pour the hot water over the whole thing. Bake 45 minutes.

At the potluck, insert a large spoon. This dessert makes its own chocolate sauce. If you happen to bring ice cream to go with it, whatever meeting you are potlucking for is bound to go smoothly.

JULY 20 ❧ WWJD

Poor Jesus. All these people wearing WWJD bracelets, wondering what a Mediterranean Jewish peasant living two thousand years ago would do, and trying to do the same thing.

It's always a good idea to interpret authoritative directions, even sacred ones, though the lens of your own century, and your own life. Love one another and love yourself are timeless rules.

Our job is to figure out what they mean today, and how to do it.

JULY 21 ❧ ELDERS AND ABILITY

I often think about my friend Christel's rubber boots. She had a pair when she lived on the farm up north. They stood by the back door, and she put them on when she went out to work in the barn or the vegetable garden. When she moved to the city, she kept the boots and wore them to work in the garden, even though there was no barn.

Now she is over 90 years old, and lives with her daughter in southern Ontario. The boots no longer stand by the back door. But she remembers them.

My own tall rubber boots disappeared a while ago. I think they may have gone tree planting, but I am not sure. I am going to buy another pair. They make me think of Christel.

JULY 22 ❧ SEIZE THE DAY

Carpe Diem, live while you can. Elders know this. Be happy in this moment, because life slips away slowly.

I don't mean that it takes time to die, although it does sometimes – my mother took several months. But the things that give us joy do not go on forever. Baby grandchildren turn into teenagers whom we adore but are hard to cuddle. The gardens we plant become too hard to weed, and the house we once filled with happy dinner parties becomes too much for us to look after.

I tell myself this, although Eli still loves stories and our arms around him, and our dinner table is often full of laughter and joy. I tell myself this when I am tempted to moan over a stiff neck or a sore toe. Seize the joy of this day, you idiot! This day! God calls us to celebrate this day! This day!

JULY 23 ❧ THE COST OF FLIGHT

I wonder if the invention of large passenger airplanes allowed many of us to fly high and decide that – oh! – there is no one up here. Our understanding of God and where God lives has changed so quickly that we can't keep up.

Mary Shelley (who wrote *Frankenstein; or, The Modern Prometheus*) would be amazed that so many novelists have emulated her fascination with the weird. Perhaps our love of zombie and vampire movies reflects a yearning for some other, any "other," to share the universe with us.

We seem to need someone to be bigger than ourselves, even if he or she is a bit bloodthirsty. It does seem sad that we took so many centuries to find our way to a loving God, only to decide that vampires are more interesting.

I was an adult before I flew in anything bigger than a bush plane. Perhaps that's why I still cling to the God of heaven and earth.

JULY 24 ❧ CATASTROPHE BOOKS

There are plenty of catastrophe books on the market – *Sea Sick: The Global Ocean in Crisis* by Alanna Mitchell, *Earth: Making a Life on a Tough New Planet* by Bill McKibben, *Collapse: How Societies Choose to Fail or Succeed* by Jared Diamond – and I read them vigorously. I know about climate change and invasive species, the dying of the sea, and the deliberate destruction by small-minded governments of the institutions set in place over many years to guard the public good.

I can't fix these things. And I just make people unhappy when I go on about what the books say. Most informed citizens of my acquaintance are pretty familiar with this stuff anyway, and they don't like it any more than I do.

I'd like to think, though, that we are all called to absorb as much as we can about the fate of our beloved and shrinking world. Then we can whisper gently about it to the neighbour who plans to vote for the guy who seems not to believe in global warming. Or we could blog about it, or organize a protest, or run for office, or run a phone or email campaign, or just put the stuff up on our Facebook page.

Or we could pray, funnelling our intentions towards health and wholeness for the city or the nation or the planet. I believe that would make a difference.

JULY 25 ❧ LIFE'S MEANING

What is the meaning of life?

I consider my father's garden and the rules for life I learned there. "Work hard. If something is worth doing, it is worth doing well." I did learn that, sometimes to my detriment.

"Fathers should talk wisely to their young daughters."

"Daughters and fathers should share in wonderful ways to care for the earth."

Later, watching my father with his grandchildren, I learned, "Grandchildren have the most fun working with a grandparent in the garden."

This is a good start to the meaning of a life.

JULY 26 ❧ NORTH AMERICAN CREATION STORIES

For many First Nations, the creator is whimsical, even mischievous, and certainly imperfect. Artist Bill Reid's magical carving, for example, of a huge raven perched on a slightly open clamshell full of struggling little creatures illuminates the humour and fear in the Haida creation story. The first men climb out of the shell and are introduced to the first women by a curious Raven, who helps them all survive even as he endlessly plays tricks on them.

Similarly, Old Man Coyote appears for some peoples as creator, for others as trickster, or both at once. In a Crow story, for instance, he encounters two ducks and enquires if there is anything in this world but water. One of them helpfully dives down and returns – eventually – with some earth, with which Old Man Coyote makes a world.

In *The Truth about Stories*, author Thomas King wonders what would have happened if the God of Genesis had been a little more understanding about the flaws of his first people; if he himself had been – well, not so perfect.

JULY 27 ❧ FROM HARMONY TO DIFFICULTY

The biblical story of Creation moves from the harmony of Eden to harshness. But North American stories often move from chaos, mud, and water towards harmony.

Paula Gunn Allen, of Laguna Pueblo and Sioux heritage, in *Grandmothers of the Light*, tells a version of the sky woman story, in which the sky woman's sorcerer husband uproots a tree and persuades her to jump through the resulting hole. Sky woman "fell so long she no longer remembered where she had come from or why she had jumped." Swans fly up to catch her, and – after a time – her grandson, named Sapling, creates the world humans live in.

Another version brings the problematic tree along. It falls into the sea and a toad swims down and salvages enough earth from it to create a world.

In Seneca artist Ernest Smith's version, the woman in the sky is curious. The Ancient Chief uproots the huge flowering tree that lights the Sky World so she can see the world below. She falls through the hole, is caught by birds and placed on the back of the turtle. A deep-diving muskrat brings up mud to form the world that we humans, her descendants, share with every other creature.

We can see how the beginning of human life is dependent on the good offices of other creatures. It makes me wonder what would have happened if European Christians, arriving in what they called – incorrectly – the New World, had been more open to the spirituality they found.

Perhaps we would understand that Adam and Eve, and us too, still live in the garden, and we need to take care of it. Perhaps the apple would be a source of marvellous knowledge, and the serpent the sign of immortality and healing that it is in some other cultures.

Perhaps we would treat water and turtles and toads with more respect.

JULY 28 ❧ THE TOWER OF BABEL

It's a fascinating story, the king of Babylon attempting to build a tower to heaven. So arrogant. In this case, the nation was scattered and many languages were formed all at once, so that no one could understand anyone else. The tower fell. How could it be built, when everyone was shouting misunderstood directions at each other?

When I am in Montreal, misusing my truly awful command of French – the loveliest of languages, I know that – I think of Babel and wish it hadn't happened.

And then I see two people talking, each choosing, as a courtesy, to speak the other's language. It works well if both are fluent. If not, you have the remarkable spectacle of two people bumbling along in a curious mix of French and English – inefficient, even ludicrous, and perfectly wonderful.

Perhaps Babel fell so that we humans could meet each other at our weakest point, at the point where we can hardly say what we mean, where we must rely on gesture and mime and the kindness of each other.

JULY 29 ❧ DREAMS WITH A VOICE

I had a dream that contained a voice speaking unambiguously. This carries great weight because it comes from the Self – the organizing principle of the whole psyche, according to Jungian analyst James Hall. This dream arrived soon after a visit with my daughter a continent away.

"You can't focus on two things at the same time." This was said twice, clearly, in different parts of the dream.

Someone wanted me to give a report on Guatemala, even though it was not on the agenda. I agreed, but needed my papers.

I gave a street urchin my old sewing machine. It and the large rusted metal trough with it were too much to carry around.

Big pronouncements usually mean just what they say. I have to focus on one thing. But what?

I've never been to Guatemala, but I have travelled in and written about other Central American countries. Guatemala, the worst in terms of death squad activity, was the one my dream chose. This dream might be asking me to look at something within me that is dying or/and it might be something linked to work as a writer.

The second part addresses my own child within, the part that infuses our adult lives with joy and sometimes sorrow. In this case the child is needy. I give it something useful from my own family (the sewing machine had been my mother's) that mends things. And I give it a large, although rusty, container for water, also very useful. These things are too heavy for me to carry from place to place anymore.

The dream may be saying that the time for my intense motherly care of my children is over. The mending and the watering as I go from place to place is feeding my own inner, hungry child, not theirs. I need to stay lovingly in touch with them, but focus on my own adult behaviour, my own work.

JULY 30 ❧ WAKING UP AT NIGHT

I am thinking more these days about the poet William Wordsworth, almost forgotten by a world that once revered him. Nothing marks me as an elder more than the fact that I can still, without flinching, cite him as an authority.

And I *am* recollecting in tranquility, just as he said. I am lying here in the dark and recognizing things I did not see at the time: That act of love; that little remark at lunch that was deep kindness; that I have been the object of pure affection from this or that person.

I think there *is* a "motion and a spirit, that impels/All thinking things, all objects of all thought,/And rolls through all things," as Wordsworth said in *Tintern Abbey*.

As an elder, I am free to rejoice in dead poets who believed in an enchanted universe. They help me remember what I need to know when I'm awake in the middle of the night.

JULY 31 ❧ NON-ANXIOUS ELDERS

Sometimes I think the most important function of an elder is to be a non-anxious presence. That calmness is useful in any volatile situation, turning the attention of the participants away from personalities and onto the issues.

It takes skill. Breathing. Love.

For me, it also involves a temptation to put such a distance between me and the situation that, although calm, I am useless, having figuratively left the room. Or the planet.

But I am learning. (Elders keep learning. That keeps us alive; we have to stay around so we can master the current skill.) What I am studying now is how to stay present and connected at the same time as I am avoiding the statement "you should...," at the same time as I am cultivating quiet in a noisy moment. Oh yes, and also allowing myself to be funny. It goes with non-anxiety.

I suppose I will have to live for a long time. I hope I can manage funny. I'm going to need it.

AUGUST 1 ❧ LAMMAS DAY

This is the time when the garden begins to lose its strength. Lammas is the first harvest festival.

In my garden, flowers are in decline from now on. It's a terrible struggle to get colour into the garden after the glorious displays of May and June and July. But it is also a time of golden afternoon light, a certain slant of the sun across the back yard that is not like any other. And it is the true beginning of the harvest. The pole beans will be coming along and maybe a few tomatoes if the transplants I put in were far enough along. There are salad crops, and herbs to add flavour to our meals.

Lammas is a good festival for elder women.

AUGUST 2 ❧ LAZY

In our immediate family, I am the child who was spared genetically caused blindness, the child who can see. I think that affected my relationship with my mother in some way. Perhaps I felt more compelled to achieve. Perhaps I then projected that compulsion onto her, blaming her for my rather work-oriented, serious personality.

It's just that children get things skewed. It is time to re-interpret what I thought as a child, lest it be passed down from one generation to another. My mother never wished guilt or high achievement on me, nor do I wish either on my children. Guilt is useless and – unless we are very careful – self-indulgent.

I might spend some time being wonderfully, guiltlessly, lazy. It makes a loving statement of its own.

AUGUST 3 ❧ ELDER YETZER HARA

Even elders get a rush of energy wanting something. It is like encountering a whole field of plump blueberries and rushing to get them before a bear or another person finds them.

The best example of *yetzer hara* in our family is the Windsor chair. It's a very nice chair, and so is the story of how we acquired it. An old residence in Quebec's Eastern Townships, where we then lived, was soon to be torn down. The furniture in it was being sold off. We knew there would be antiques at bargain prices for the fleet of foot.

My husband – not normally an antique hound, but learning – lined up early the morning of the sale. As soon as the doors opened he flew up the stairs and grabbed the Windsor chair. Holding it in his arms, he rushed over to sit on a fine birds-eye maple chest, thereby snagging two pieces at once.

All the way up the stairs he could hear panting behind him, but he was much too fast for his pursuers. For years afterwards, one of them delighted in telling us each time we met how "that damned United Church minister" had beaten her to the objects of her desire.

The chair has been a fixture in our dining room for 35 years now. I never fail to feel a little jolt of pleasure when I see its curved and graceful lines. It was a little defeat for too-bright saintliness, a loosening of the mask of goodness that might have been a bit tight, a little victory for the hunter within who must sometimes be indulged.

AUGUST 4 ❧ MINIATURIZATION

As my mother grew more frail, my once-large world shrank to our house, her nursing home, and side trips to church or the grocery store. This was not an unwelcome triangle. There was a holy calm about it.

My head knew this would not last. But my heart went back to the same place it had been the last time I was pregnant. I knew that I would give birth one day. But as the months went by and I became accustomed to my rounded shape, I began to contemplate the possibility that I would stay this way forever, that my world would always consist mostly of me and the one-who-was-on-the-way. So it was with my mother's months of dying. Perhaps my world would be miniaturized forever.

In both instances, birth and death, there was hesitation and anticipation. Hesitation because this peaceful, sacred interlude, once over, would not come again. Anticipation because there would be newness of life at the end.

I hadn't thought about newness of life when my mother first began to leave us. By the end I knew that she would find it. Her last gift to me, from her tiny world, was this bulwark for my own dying.

AUGUST 5 ⁊ BERWICK

One summer Jim and I led the morning Bible studies at Berwick Camp, a summer encampment in Nova Scotia with a long-standing tradition of scholarship and inspiration. We had worked hard to prepare, and even while there we were revising and rewriting each afternoon after our two hours of sessions in the morning.

Our reward was increasing numbers of people turning up each morning. By the last day we were speaking to about a hundred people. We asked them to write a poem.

We were quite nervous about this, although we did our best to appear confident. Many people do not like to write poems, and indeed feel they cannot. We gave them the first line: *You took me by surprise, God*, and asked for six more lines. We gave them five minutes to write.

In the recess between the sessions we quickly chose some to read aloud. As far as we could tell, every single person had written a poem. They were startling, moving, raw, vulnerable, and often joyous.

All week long these people had been living in a safe and loving environment, under ancient trees, listening attentively each evening to our friend Peter Short's brilliant sermons. The children played around the cottages, the elders sat on their tiny porches and chatted, the little cookie cabin dispensed free cookies all day, as many as you liked. The meals were alarmingly good, and so was the music. In fact, we were living in Eden.

Perhaps all this together made these poems so good: the example of Peter's marvellous language, the protection of the trees, the sense that God was near, the singing. It meant that a bunch of folk on holiday wrote about God with intimacy and clarity.

We read the poems aloud as well as we could, into intense silence. How much would these poems ripple into the rest of their lives? we wondered. Who might be so touched by another's poem that they would react kindly in a conflict or vote differently in an election?

How much can a poem change the world?

AUGUST 6 ❧ HIROSHIMA DAY

People in many cities float paper lanterns marked with peace messages on water today to mark Hiroshima Day. August 6, 1945 was the day a nuclear device exploded over the Japanese city of Hiroshima. Two days later, the citizens of Nagasaki met the same fate.

The little floating lights remind us that peace is important. They are like the eight candles of the *Hanukkiya* lit later in the year to remind us of a miracle; and the four candles of Advent that remind us God is coming.

At any First Nations gathering a sacred fire, which must not go out until the meeting is over, is lit. Diwali, the autumn Hindu festival of light celebrates the victory of good over evil. On Christmas Eve our neighbours make paper-bag-and-candle luminaria to line the streets around us with light in the winternight.

Small flames, light in the darkness, hope. This is what it is to be human.

AUGUST 7 ❦ DREAMS OF DRIVING

I had this dream one night, after I had been worrying about the way I was attempting to be helpful to a grown-up child. Car dreams often indicate the manner in which we are going through life. In this case, my worrying had unknowingly posed the question for the dream before I fell asleep.

We were going the wrong way on a roundabout. Someone else was driving. "Just pull over and stop for a bit," I called, but the driver wouldn't do that.

Clearly, in terms of being a good mom, I was going (round) about this the wrong way. This short but value-packed dream even offered the solution. "Just pull over and stop for a bit."

It's hard for a mother to do. I woke up, wrote it down, and fell asleep again, to a dream in which I couldn't find my ringing phone. When I did find it, *I couldn't answer it. All I could get was an old message from my mother.*

Dreams will often come in series in case you don't get the idea the first time. This second dream, immediately following the "wrong way" dream suggests, I think, that I was functioning out of "old messages" from my mother. But, says the dream firmly, that is not an answer.

A few more dreams followed. (It was a busy night.) The final one was of a big party at our house, with *so many relatives it seemed like a wonderful, happy café.*

I think that is a promise that the problem will be solved.

AUGUST 8 ❧ AUTHENTICITY

One of the pleasures of being an elder is that you have had time to get to know some people very well. I have known my husband for 48 years. Although I have had to be stern with him about broadcasting this fact – for some obscure reason he likes to announce to flight attendants that we have been married for 45 years as we get on a plane – mostly we like each other immensely. We know each other well. I savour his virtues of honesty and authenticity, even as I order him not to detail for strangers the peculiar length of our relationship.

In his turn he admires me. At least he says so. (You can see I have a stake in his being honest.) When I ask for details he recites a list of virtues. He has reservations about only one trait. "Oh, and you're very...reclusive," he concludes.

He is not. On any canoe trip lasting more than a day, he takes to greeting strangers with delight, even if they are in a boat on the far side of a lake. "Hellooo," he shouts, waving his paddle madly. "Hellooo!"

A new someone to talk to, who has not heard any of his stories and who just might want to know how long we have been married. What if, I have suggested to him, what if that is an entire boat full of introverts, all recluses just like me? What if you are the only extrovert on this lake?

I know him very well.

AUGUST 9 ❧ ELDER ANGER

From my journal at the time:

We have just moved my mother from assisted living to long-term care. She fought it until there was no point in further resistance. Even with a care worker four times a day, she needed two people to help her to the bathroom. So we had the cab that was equipped for wheelchairs come and make the official move, all of it fraught beforehand with paperwork and tension (would there be a room? Would there be a private room? How much would it cost?). It took days and days to get ready.

My mother is not grateful to me at all but at least she has not erupted again with her earlier pain-filled statement: "You just want to put me in a nursing home so you can travel."

I left in tears.

My mother is overwhelmingly angry. She doesn't like her new place ("they don't like me here," a projection if I ever heard it) and I believe her remarks to some of the staff are genuinely abusive. She doesn't greet me when I come in, just demands to know "Where are my…?" fill in the blank. Yesterday it was her socks. They were down in the laundry being labelled. But then she calms down and asks for forgiveness for being so cranky, admits the meals are very good, and the whirlpool bath a luxury. And I calm down too, and consider anger and courage, and how deeply they are related.

Anger and survival – you can't untangle them. You can't have one without the other.

AUGUST 10 ❧ CARING FOR CREATION

How can religious bodies care for Creation? First, they could learn to love it. They could have some church services out of doors, quitting the sanctuary and pews maybe four times a year.

The outreach committee of our church considers the care of Mother Earth to be its mission. The church hosts meetings of green groups and animates the rest of the congregation to arrive at city hall when need be. Even the frailest elder can fill a seat in the Council chambers. Speakers offer after-church forums on energy saving and living simply and other good efforts. Worship underpins it all. Many hymnbooks are full of songs that celebrate the loveliness of the earth. Our prayers are full of similar joy.

We know that God's house is not just the building, crucial though it is to hosting our efforts. God lives in the forest and the lake as well, and we expect to find God there.

AUGUST 11 ❧ HOLLYHOCKS

More and more, as an elder, I feel a responsibility to welcome the spirits of the past. Our hollyhocks, for instance, remind Jim and me of his mother, who always grew them in her small garden. When ours are in bloom – as now – memories crowd around and nudge us. Jim's mother had a gentle but highly accurate wit, as has her son, my husband. It was passed on to our son and now, I think, our grandson.

Wit is the unexpected conjunction of two unrelated ideas, produced at just the right moment. It is tricky – a witty remark has to be made quickly, in the moment, and with all appearance of innocence. It requires quick thinking. Introverts – myself included – don't do wit well, because we wait and think over what we are about to say, and by then it is too late.

Eli did a junior witticism last winter, as I was briskly moving him into his snowsuit. "How many scarves," he inquired, "would a giraffe need?"

But this is summer and the hollyhocks, purple and pink and red, stand tall at the back of the garden bed. It is too shady for them there so they have a tendency to lean drunkenly and I have to stake them unobtrusively. They are subject to rust, and I have to strip off the lacy yellowed lower leaves and put them into the garbage, not the compost pile. I don't want the whole yard to be infected.

But I would never stop growing them. Eli needs to know about his great-grandmother. She would have loved the giraffe.

AUGUST 12 ❧ OFFICIAL PLANS

Most Canadian cities have one. They are generally mind-numbing, but important. They lay out in detail the vision your city has for its future. Provinces review them to make sure they are in line with provincial policies about the way cities will look.

So far, so good.

Unfortunately, official plans are often weaker than they appear. They can be amended easily, and in any case, they do not have the force of law. They constitute a vision, not a blueprint.

But for community groups who are seeking to save parks or heritage buildings, water supply or wetlands, they can be extremely useful, because they do contain – even if in vague and insubstantial statements – the best intentions of the planners.

Elders are often members of those conserving community groups. That's because we have the time to be involved. It takes days to digest an official plan, but it is worth it. Our job as citizens is to save the best of our civic space for our grandchildren, or at least, someone's grandchildren. We hope that another elder is doing the same for the city or town or village or rural area in which our own, or someone's, grandchildren live.

Elders have time for planning.

AUGUST 13 ❧ NUISANCE VALUE

I remember when I was a teenager. (Doesn't everyone? It was as emotionally fraught then as it is now.) My friends pulled me aside one day and told me I would never get a boyfriend. I laughed too loud and I was too smart.

I failed geometry, and set out, unsuccessfully, to develop a more elegant laugh. My peers and my parents were raising me to be polite and unobtrusive.

It's quite difficult to overcome that early training. But the other day my grandson said, "Nana, I love your laugh!" He's four. He likes my laugh, the louder and more uncontrolled the better.

It's too late for geometry, but it's not too late to unlearn automatic politeness. By all means, I need to be respectful. Respect is something deeper than manners; it is the recognition of your opponent as a human being with a right to dignity. But slowly – slowly – I am learning to let go of the need to stifle laughter.

AUGUST 14 ❧ PICKING TOMATOES

A h! This is the month for whole wheat fresh brown bread and big slices of fresh-off-the-vine tomato. Eli picks the cherry tomatoes into a bowl and we eat them as they are.

He thinks he doesn't like tomatoes. And who would, for the rest of the year? But right now, this month and next, the gift of Peruvian gods makes it paradise.

We celebrate.

AUGUST 15 ❧ TALKING

I find I talk with my father in the garden more than I used to. He's been dead for more than 25 years. I don't talk out loud, just in my head, asking where I should put this plant or that.

I am beginning to allow my mother into my mind as well. We had a difficult time with boundaries, she and I, so much so that the last great wall of her dying took awhile to overcome. But now I can begin to feel the happiness she would have felt when one of her grandchildren appears, and the pleasure she took in colour and design even when she couldn't see.

All this is good. Except when some not-so-helpful affirmation is handed down through the generations. You should always have a large turkey at Christmas. Everyone should be married by the time they are thirty. Mothers should not work outside the home. It's best to know your place.

That's when talking to the ancestors and explaining that this has to change is helpful. Elders can do that, but not out loud, unless they are alone.

AUGUST 16 ❧ FIRST NATIONS VALUES

When I covered events involving First Nations people, I soon discovered that when the circle forms, reporters are not left out. It was expected I would participate like everyone else. Once, when headlines were flaring over events at Kahnewake, I found myself offering the closing benediction at a Mohawk meeting. It was not an attempt on their part to compromise my reporting. It was recognition that even journalists are spiritual beings. They left nobody out. They made sure all were included.

There is a distinct bias in many First Nations towards unwritten recollection – which works because participants pay intense attention. It was respectfully suggested at one meeting that I might want to refrain from taking notes. So I did. It was extremely hard work. And I found that when I did write up my notes after each session, they were already sorted in my head.

I knew what was crucial in a way that normally required some time to figure out.

Inclusion. Attention. Respect. These are not empty words with First Nations people. I experienced them first-hand. I would like to suggest overhauling all our decision-making processes, at every level of government in Canada, in order to make them more First Nations.

AUGUST 17 ❧ WHAT WAS LEFT BEHIND?

When an elder retires, a question arises: What part of me that has been left behind now wants to be picked up? As a writer who worked slowly and needed a lot of thinking time, I found it necessary to protect my required solitary time. So maybe it is now my time to have time for everyone, to learn how to pause and simply enjoy the moment of visiting.

If the elder's previous work was heavy in the other direction – as a social worker for instance, or a priest or minister, whose life was spent making room for people – it might be beneficial to relax and find ways to enjoy being alone.

The second half of life involves compensating for the first until you are a whole and complete person.

AUGUST 18 ❧ THE SATURDAY FARMERS' MARKET

At our Saturday farmers' market you can get fresh whole wheat bread and pecan pie and butter tarts. You can buy baby perennials that are already accustomed to our part of the world, and glossy zucchini, and raspberries; whatever is in season. I nudge my extroverted husband along, handing him baskets of berries and fresh bread to carry while he visits joyfully with people we do not see at other times.

Markets like this are appearing all over the country.

The farmers' market is the new town centre, says author Michael Pollan (*The New York Review of Books*, June 10, 2010). Buying locally is yearly more widespread. It is changing the way we think as consumers, Pollan says, a new attitude towards food that is putting "the relationship between consumers and producers on a new, more neighborly footing…and encouraging us to regard our food dollars as 'votes' for a different kind of agriculture and, by implication, economy."

I think about the fresh eggs my parents bought from local farmers when I was small, and the cheese, oh yes, the cheese. My parents boxed it up and sent it to me sometimes when I was away at university, and it was rich and tasted of home.

Maybe not so new. Maybe this is what elders knew in their childhood, coming back to life.

AUGUST 19 ❧ PERFECT OR NOT

I remember my father cutting scabs off the potatoes he grew. There was some virus in the soil of his garden that he couldn't eradicate. No matter how skillfully he fertilized and watered, no matter how friable the soil from all the manure and compost he dug in, his potatoes had scars on them. They were never perfect – although they tasted wonderful.

It's a good memory for us to have now. We have all been damaged by perfect, pesticide-laden food. We think if we can't produce picture-book produce, then there is no use in trying.

I struggle therefore, when I grow beans and peas, tomatoes and Swiss chard, to be unalarmed by the occasional hole in the leaves or a bean that gets out of control and, unpicked, grows large and rock-hard. (That one just goes on the compost, since beans produce so heavily you can never keep up.)

It's true. Perfection is the enemy of the good.

AUGUST 20 ❧ WRITING TIP

I am writing this book on faith. I do not always know what I going to say or whether it will come out right. Yet I wake up at night full of thoughts and ideas, and run to get a paper and pen to write them down. I must talk about how I have experienced the love of friends, how important it is for elders to seize the day and heal the world.

The thoughts that come at night are the ones that can't push through the assumptions of daylight. They need quiet to be heard.

Never discount the value of the pen and notebook beside the bed. A flashlight is a kindness if you have a partner.

AUGUST 21 ❧ TREES

We used to have two massive white spruces at the back of the yard. They cut the strongest winds and helped keep our beloved shady maple safe.

A couple of years ago we had a storm with twisting winds that broke the top forty feet off one spruce and threw it into our neighbour's yard. It didn't land on anything. This several-ton piece of wood found a diagonal landing spot in the only place that avoided crushing our fence or the neighbour's garage. Telephone and hydro repair people re-stringing fallen lines the next day found this miraculous (or words to that effect).

The same storm dropped a tree belonging to our other neighbours into our back yard. Trees were down all over. The whole neighbourhood spent convivial days cutting off branches, attacking fallen trunks with chainsaws, and hauling what we didn't want to the curb. Our family received excellent pastoral care from friends in other parts of the city, who had rushed to make sure the big maple was okay.

The remnant of the big spruce still stands in our back yard. Ivy has grown up it, smothering its remaining sixty feet of now-dead tree trunk with green, and offering a home to birds. It shields the maple from heavy winds as it has always done.

I don't wish for more storms. I do wish we always gathered like this to love the trees together.

AUGUST 22 ❧ DIFFERENT IN THE DARK

We wake up. Perhaps something aches. And then, lying in the dark, fresh from a dream, we are sometimes assaulted by another perspective, one that we had not considered.

It is not that one perspective is right and the other wrong. It is that we need to take both into account and integrate them, make them whole.

The shadow – that part of our unconscious most deeply hidden from us – is a very helpful concept. We need always to seek out that part of ourselves that we don't know, that part of our story that we put away when we were young. Then we can make it part of our daily decisions and lead a life of wholeness, including aches.

AUGUST 23 ❧ FIRST NATIONS ELDERS

My friend Aaron has been learning his Anishinabe culture. His father is First Nations; his mother, and my dear wise friend, is not. Aaron is spending time with an elder in his First

Nation as well as studying post-graduate law, absorbing and integrating the richness of both cultures within his own person.

I asked him about the concept of elders in the Anishinabe community. I was hoping to enlarge the concept of "elder" in my own culture where the term "old" is often derogatory.

For one thing, Aaron explained, the authority held by the elder is much larger and more far-reaching. While an elder in my own culture might be respected within a family or circle of friends, in Anishinabe culture they are "speakers for the community and culture," with "interpretive authority over the stories, and how they are conveyed."

The stories are very important. The elders lend legitimacy to events, opening and closing gatherings, with a power unapproached by any keynote speaker at any convention we might hold. And they are treated with great respect. If you must disagree with an elder, "you have to find a way to contradict them without challenging their authority."

Most elders are old. But an elder is not necessarily old. Being an elder has to do with "the way you exist in the world," he says. It has to do with "leading a good life, with the acquisition of a certain world view that generally comes only with age."

Aaron smiles. "It has to do with the depth with which you understand the connection of all things," he says. "It sounds simple. But it's not."

This is a long way from the attack ads that are aimed at the respected leaders in our own culture who run for public office. I wish that we could learn this concept of an elder; I wish that we could carry it in our hearts. I wish that we understood how deeply we are all connected, rich with poor, humans with other creatures, all living things with water and trees and rocks.

AUGUST 24 ❧ DREAMS OF CLOTHES

Dreams will return again and again, circling around in different forms until they get our attention. I believe this dream is warning me to do the work of my old age before it is too late.

I was at someone's cottage. It was very beautiful but not my own, although I longed to fix it up and change things around.

I had brought only the clothes I was wearing and a large bag that contained some kind of contraband, and was empty at the bottom. I was dressed in elegant slacks perhaps for a wedding.

But maybe I could borrow some clothes from the very elderly owner, who was not staying overnight.

I was standing looking out over the water. I loved this place. But the water was bitter cold and I was standing at the edge of a cliff, very close to the edge.

It is time to enjoy the world's wonders – lakes, rocks, trees – which I love ("the cottage"). But I have not yet taken ownership of my old age; I am still wearing the clothes ("elegant slacks") that symbolize my earlier, more career-driven life. Perhaps I am still seeking the integration (the "wedding") and balance that is the struggle of the working woman (and man). Indeed, judging by the "contraband" hidden in "the large bag" I am still propelled by un-examined secrets in my unconscious. But maybe – my dream sug-gests – maybe I could let this baggage go and try on the clothes/role of eldership. Because the bitter cold waters of death are not so far away, the dream warns. I am just at the cliff's edge.

We have been postponing a long-planned, week-long camping trip. Somehow, last summer was too short. I think this year we must pack our tent and go.

AUGUST 25 ❧ RELIGIOUS PEOPLE

Increasingly, religious people are seen as naïve, innocent, de-luded, or conniving. In fact, I am inclined to feel that some religious people of a more fundamentalist leaning than my own are conniving. I fear (with author Marci McDonald, in *The Ar-mageddon Factor: The Rise of Christian Nationalism in Canada*) that some religious allies of the Conservative party envision the country adhering to strict fundamentalist values, "governed by biblical literalists."

It's hard to see any nuance here. The Conservatives banished long-established government funding from KAIROS, the church coalition that brought aid to the poorest of the poor in Africa. It was difficult to fathom why. Was it that KAIROS also brought an effort to provide human rights? Was it that the organization is a creation of the mainline churches, those that do not anticipate Armageddon arising out of the Middle East?

Perhaps we are now caught in a covert religious war between those who use metaphor and symbol to describe a God who loves Creation, and those who see God literally as a fierce judge soon to be bringing about the end times.

I don't mind at all if I am considered naïve. But it is important for elders to be clear about which God we serve.

AUGUST 26 ❧ POLITICAL BULLIES

It is all of a piece. Bullying in the House of Commons and bullying nature by exploiting the tar sands. Elders should be able to see through this. Elders need to pick up their dignity and stand in front of any politician who is rude.

When one of our city councillors treated another councillor – a green-friendly one – to a series of humiliating remarks at a public meeting, our little group of environmentalists watched in horror.

The next day my husband wrote a careful letter to the bully in question, outlining what he had seen and why it was wrong. He took it to his place of business and presented his letter.

"Your behaviour," he said bluntly, "was unacceptable."

The councillor – confronted by an elder – was contrite.

Elders have nothing to lose. Nobody can fire us. And sometimes people are so shocked when we call them to account they actually listen.

AUGUST 27 ❧ TRAFFIC

Here's a dilemma. Our city plans to widen one of its long residential streets within the next few years, making it much more travelled. One segment of the street is old and very narrow. Widening the street would be devastating for the little neighbourhood along its way. Some would have traffic roaring by their front steps.

Hard decisions are ahead. If it becomes clear the plan will be activated, each resident will have to decide whether to get out while the going is good, or stay and fight for the serenity of their homes. The financial cost of staying might be significant. The cost to the soul of seeing a collection of lovely old homes defeated by cars is definitely significant.

AUGUST 28 ❧ TREES

The neighbourhood plans to lobby against widening their street. The city engineer is a good listener, so they hope their points will be heard:

There is insufficient room for the boulevards that should be part of every busy roadway.

Without boulevards, roadside trees and shrubs can't be planted, and the neighbourhood would lose its mature urban tree cover.

Increased traffic would split one side of the road from the other. Front yard gardeners would have to shout at one another above the noise, trying to tell each other how nice their roses look.

There would be no room for roses.

It is hard not to rant. Why, I want to know, would any municipality destroy a neighbourhood that functions very well for the sake of moving traffic a little faster? Traffic moves too quickly already. Some drivers routinely go 60 or 70 kilometres per hour in a zone that boasts three schools.

Aside from safety is the issue of beauty. Why would the city create ugliness – the removal of shade trees – when something attractive already exists? Why is this city not doing as Montreal does, and demanding a maximum speed of 40 kilometres per hour in residential neighbourhoods? Why not install removable concrete planters full of flowers mid-street to force drivers to slow down? Anyone going too quickly is likely to lose a bumper, which strikes me as a fine idea. A bumper is easier to replace than a child.

Why are cars more important than people?

AUGUST 29 ❧ DINNER MEMORIES

Sometimes I have offered bits of china to my children. Generally they say no, which always surprised me. I thought we had a lot of happy memories from meal times, and they would welcome the chance to integrate them into their lives.

Then I visited them in their homes, and realized how the plate on which the food that nourishes your guests is served is a remarkable personal choice. It reflects who you are. And they are not their parents. I was proud of this insight. However – foolishly – I made one last effort to pass on a large inheritance of dishes.

"No thank you," was the polite response. Then came the happy reminiscence I had longed for. "I have my own dishes. But could I have the table?"

AUGUST 30 ❧ UNSAID IN THE BIRTHING ROOM

They don't tell you this.

The line between us will stretch across a country
and it's far.

First the long lean into the crib
then across the room
a city-length away to school

and now this flat continent
    and sea.

I wonder how this distance came to be?

We meet by phone and it is not enough
Two women, equals, friends

but

Was I good enough as mother?
Was there time enough?

We peeled apples
And I listened –
Didn't I?

And then you were gone.

But we all grow up
don't we?
We all grow old and stretch our hearts to death
across these continents of time.

AUGUST 31 ❧ JUSTICE

On television, a news story. Twenty years after her frozen body was found in a shed, police have found the man who killed a thirteen-year-old Winnipeg girl, Candace Derksen.

I watch in tears. Her mother, Wilma Derksen, had spoken to me almost that long ago about the loss of her daughter and her own attempts to find a way to forgive and go on. I was writing a piece about restorative justice.

In the midst of her anguish, Wilma Derksen had become active in the movement to bring restorative justice to Canada's correctional services. She visited offenders – murderers – in prison and spoke to them about the cost to her family, about the immeasurable pain their actions had caused, about her wish for them to see and acknowledge what they had done so that forgiveness could be possible and the community restored to harmony.

That is what "restorative" justice is about. Not punishment, but the restoration of humanity to a killer who has taken leave of it; the possibility of forgiveness for a family that has endured impossible pain; the restoration of harmony to a society that is wounded and in chaos.

Wilma Derksen is deeply, profoundly respected by the people she visited and the organizations who called her to speak to their members.

And now her daughter's killer has been found. Derksen spoke to the cameras with consummate dignity, neither hiding her suffering nor demanding retribution. She carried an armload of white roses, and she and her husband and their family and friends placed them gently on Candace's grave.

Justice and reconciliation. They go together. Onlookers cannot do it. Only those who have been damaged can offer forgiveness to the offender; and only after the offender acknowledges and repents of what he or she has done. Restitution, as much as possible, must be made.

We should remember this, when the question of Indian residential schools comes up. Because in that case, as citizens of Canada, we are all the offenders.

SEPTEMBER 1 ❧ THE MONTH OF RETURN

The state of Israel has a policy called the right of return. If you are Jewish, anywhere in the world, you can become a citizen of Israel. You can return to the place whose collective memory is in your bones, no matter how far in the past that was.

September is my month of return. I always feel a little sad because the holidays are over, even though I am on permanent holiday now. The "holidays" for which my bones mourn are the two months of school holidays, even though neither I nor my children have been in school for many years. But I remember.

The sadness is mixed with pleasure in what remains. The trees are still fully leaved and some flowers persist. Familiar children from the neighbourhood walk by on their way to school with comforting predictability.

Everything about this month is precious, despite the tattered edges. The plants in the garden have been gnawed at by various critters, and the salad garden has holes in it where I didn't get around to replanting. The crabapple trees are laden with bright red fruit, which I should pick and make into jelly, but I don't.

Instead I sit on the deck, reading, in the last bit of summer warmth. We use the barbecue for everything possible, including an attempt – partly successful – to make biscuits on it. We eat outside for every meal, including breakfast.

I don't need to be productive. I am returned to myself, at peace.

SEPTEMBER 2 ❧ A PRAYER FOR SEPTEMBER

God of Earth's beauty, we give you thanks, and
Blessings on your hovering red-tinged leaves, which we admire,
Blessings on the pole beans, which we taste with joy,
Blessings on the open lake, the sand, the ducks, the loons, the picnics
*   by the shore.*
Blessings on it all.

God of Earth's beauty, we give you thanks, and
Blessings on the future snows to come, in which we like to play,
Blessings on the crowded city streets and shops and plays and films,
Blessings on your future festivals of light, the sparkling trees and gifts,
*   the songs.*
Blessings on us all.
Amen.

SEPTEMBER 3 ❧ RETROSPECTION

Old age is a good time to look back and see why things happened the way they did, and what shaped us.

It's not easy to do. But it might take the focus off the usual suspects when we want to blame someone else for the way we are. If we can figure out why we are fearful or sad, distrustful or too eager to please, we might be able to change.

Even at this late date, that inner work could shift the entire family towards a necessary change. Generation after generation people make mistakes that arise out of the same factors.

But families do things right from one generation to another too. Family dynasties of helping professionals could be the result of a strong family ethos that no one feels able to leave, or – better – the result of learning within the family how to be healing towards all its members. Each child picks up the special skills.

It may not mean they all become doctors and nurses and midwives and therapists. It just means their presence in the world, in whatever they do, is positive.

Retrospection can determine strengths as well as weaknesses, and then you can let them show so others can receive them.

SEPTEMBER 4 ❧ OLD ELI

When vision is lacking, societal change requires an alliance between the young and very old. That is why the relationship between grandparents and grandchildren is so important. The child Samuel in the biblical story hears God's voice; but his elder, old Eli, is needed to interpret what is going on.

I am sleeping warm, protected,
something whispers in my mind;
and sighing through the blackness,
speaks my name upon the wind.

It is a time of seldom dreaming
when all the grownups' hearts are cold,
and the future we are promised
has grown tired and very old.

Who would make this quiet murmur?
I am startled wide-awake.
Must be Eli, old and fragile
and I hasten, for his sake.
It's a time of seldom dreaming
when the grownups cannot hear;
but the children keep the magic,
listen still with open ears.
But old Eli tells me, "Samuel,
it was not my voice you heard
like an echo through the blackness,
but the whisper of our Lord."
It is a time of seldom dreaming
when the grownups cannot see;
but I am young so I remember
how the world was planned to be.

I return to wait in silence
for the holy, three-in-one.
Then I hear God's voice explaining
Eli's sons have done much wrong
and the young must tell the old ones,
God will give us language strong
to tell how farms are laid with concrete
and the whales have lost their song.

It is the work of our young vision,
to show the oil that coats the sea,
and the soil blown from the prairies
and the rain that kills the trees.
If the grownups join our dreaming
God will grant another start.
We can begin to fix Creation
when they waken from the dark.

SEPTEMBER 5 ❧ FROM TAXPAYER TO CITIZEN

When our GreenSpace group was struggling to save parks in our city, we always referred to ourselves as "citizens" (signifying our desire for wholeness and transparency in civic life) when we addressed the (now-former) city council. Most of them referred to us as "taxpayers," (signifying their desire to appeal to voters on only one level, their pocketbooks).

And then one week – after we had stalled yet another effort to sell parkland to a developer – we noticed the mayor using the word "citizen." He knew which way the wind was blowing.

If you work hard enough at the language, you can begin to change the political discourse, making sure that considerations like beauty and health are taken into account along with finding what is most cost-effective.

You know the language of dissent is working when the opposition starts using your words.

SEPTEMBER 6 ❧ A PAIN IN THE NECK

My physiotherapist is making me stand up straight. At five feet nine inches tall, I learned early on to stoop for the sake of many of the guys I danced with in high school. Later, as a writer, I hunched intently into my stories. That's when I wasn't tucking my phone between my neck and my ear, so I could write and turn pages while I interviewed someone. I still read a lot, bent over a book.

Lately I am hearing a weird sound, like a drum roll, when I turn my head. Rattle rattle rattle. And it hurts. So now, at my late age, I am lifting weights and doing lunges, and keeping my head lifted up like a turtle coming out of its shell. And trying to put my shoulder blades in my back pockets.

I am walking tall and straight like the beautiful Luo women I stayed with once in Kenya, who carried large containers of water on their heads for kilometres and had no need of physiotherapy.

SEPTEMBER 7 ❧ ADVICE, RE-THOUGHT

I sent this message to all my children today. I know, elders really should wait until advice is solicited. But I felt this fell under the rubric of elder privilege. Just this once.

Memo from Mother to all of you. Maintain core strength. And do not slouch as I have done my whole life, to my (now) deep regret!!

It's all right to distribute advice if it arises out of very painful experience. And it is never too late (or too early) to walk tall.

SEPTEMBER 8 ❧ DIAMOND EARRINGS

One of my sons gave me earrings a long time ago, when he was little. I was already a little bent over from my work.

My middle son
gave me diamond earrings for Christmas.
Not real ones – his budget
doesn't stretch to that –
just little chips of crystal
that glow in my ears like diamonds.

My middle son
hasn't noticed
I wear jeans
all the time.
That I'm tall,
and awkward,
and stooped a little
from too much fussing over manuscripts.

He thinks I should wear diamonds.
So I do.

SEPTEMBER 9 ✢ HOMES AND HOUSES

When I was in grade nine French class, we read *Le Notaire du Havre*, by Georges Duhamel. It gave me a glimpse of a different culture. In the story, the civil servant in question was raising his family in an apartment building. I found this extremely strange. Before you laugh, consider that I was living in a very small town. There were no apartment buildings.

But our twelve-year-old selves stay with us. I was shocked, later, into an appreciation of life in high-density downtown Toronto, where I went to university. But my image of "home" as a detached, single-family dwelling never budged. *Le notaire* remained a strange, pitiable, European creature forced to live away from the ground with no lawn of his own.

Until our little grandson moved into a condo in downtown Montreal, where he delighted in fountains and city parks and massive conference centres. One cold Sunday we spent a whole enchanted morning exploring the city's deserted underground, a marvel of elegant brickwork and art installations, sky-lit restaurants, and more fountains.

My image of the good life, created in childhood, began to crack and break open. Just in time. Now we are discovering the terrible trap of wide-open suburban life for elders, who must eventually give up driving their cars and discover they can no longer shop for groceries or get to the library.

Just in time, I have given up the lawn.

SEPTEMBER 10 ❦ DREAMS OF FIRE

When change is taking place within, dreams point it out. Change can be frightening, and the dream reassures us. One agent of transformation we are all familiar with is fire. That symbol appears in this dream, which arrived just over a year after my retirement.

I dreamed about a house Jim bought and to which he was building an addition. Although I was uneasy, I said nothing. Then there were lots of people in the house; it seemed to be a long apartment building with a huge inner courtyard, with flowers and a curving long walkway with paving stones, very pretty. The whole thing was just one storey.

Then someone came with a delivery. He left a package, but he also started throwing clothes around, and they began to burn. There were small fires inside and outside.

Someone called the fire department but it took awhile for it to arrive. A very old battered truck came eventually. It drove past and I wondered how we would call it back, but it turned and arrived at the house. Firemen began to put water on the fires, but only on the outside fires.

A large crowd came and toasted marshmallows. Meantime, a man started setting the house next door on fire. Nobody seemed worried about anything.

Apparently Donna-as-wife (the "house that Jim bought") has only "one story." A new narrative of my existence needs to be created. I do have a "very pretty" inner life. Perhaps that makes me unwilling to embark on necessary change.

So the agent of change (the delivery man) arrives and begins dismantling my earlier roles ("throwing clothes around" which begin to "burn"). I seem to have found some emotional heat. Perhaps some passion – for justice, for writing, for beauty – is at last beginning to heat up. Perhaps I have been a teeny bit bored, but "uneasy" about taking on something fresh.

The relaxed way my dream-ego regards these fires – the truck doesn't hurry, then it goes past, and finally people start roasting marshmallows, for heaven's sake – would indicate that the fires are not unwelcome. ("Nobody seemed worried.")

Sociologist Sara Lawrence-Lightfoot points out in *The Third Chapter* that this elder time is meant "to bring the pieces together and make ourselves whole..." and it is "more difficult and demanding than the learning we have experienced at earlier stages in our lives..."

It is time, this dream seems to be saying. Get on with life.

SEPTEMBER 11 ❧ WHY RELIGION?

Radio phone-in callers and television debaters all wonder: What use is religion when it has done so much harm?

And yet, Karen Armstrong explains in *The Great Transformation: The Beginning of Our Religious Traditions*, the spiritual traditions embraced by most of humanity today began "as principled and visceral recoil from the unprecedented violence of their time."

Confucianism, Daoism, Hinduism, Buddhism, the notion of one God that led to rabbinic Judaism and Christianity and Islam, the flowering of Greek philosophy in Plato and Aristotle – all these developed in a war-riven period of seven centuries. From 900 to 200 BCE, in four separate regions of the world – China, India, Israel, and Greece – sages concluded that self-emptying, love, kindness, generosity, and above all compassion were the means by which humans could live together without destroying themselves.

Each collection of the world's peoples arrived at a new vision. Ethical behaviour and deep benevolence, deep care for the other

– *every* other – leads humans to a transcendent encounter with the divine and stops us from self-destruction.

That vision is terribly hard. Every religion diluted it and moved away from the great vision of the Axial sages. But when people complain that religion has done nothing but harm, we should remember that its *intention* was to heal. Later generations, attempting to put the great faiths into practice, messed up a good thing.

It's not too late to remember what the sages knew.

SEPTEMBER 12 ❧ TRANSITION TOWNS

The new global movement called Transition Towns is attempting to help us deal with peak oil. They want us to create more sustainable communities with less focus on imported strawberries in January. They want to help us make the transition to a much less fossil-fuel-dependent life.

And perhaps it would be a happier life as well. Theologian Doug Hall describes "covert" despair as a familiar emotion in industrialized countries. Despair you hardly know you are feeling, despair that is hidden from our conscious selves, like a vast pit beneath our feet, glimpsed from time to time and swiftly banished from our minds.

In poorer countries, despair may be more overt. Of course we despair when we cannot feed our children. There is nothing hidden or covert about it. But in our country, we despair quietly, unconsciously, because the water grows less drinkable, the climate changes, the soil is damaged, the habitat for other creatures becomes more fractured, and we don't know how to help.

There is hope coming, though. At our last Transition Town potluck supper, someone wondered how to start a car-sharing program. Our yard-sharing program (to grow vegetables) is underway. An expert is coming to talk with us about solar panels.

Maybe we won't need all this. Maybe the oil will flow freely forever.

But these are young people. Their little children enliven the potluck suppers. We can all see their future coming. We aren't taking a chance on that.

SEPTEMBER 13 ❧ RUDBECKIA

They used to bloom only in the fall in my garden, but they self-seed ridiculously and now the new little plants are liable to burst into bloom anytime from July on. They look like a child's drawing of the sun, a brown disk in the middle with yellow rays shooting out all around.

My favourite are called *rudbeckia hirta* (hairy) because their stems are fuzzy; I can pick them and put them in big bouquets around the house where they whisper cunningly, for a long time, "The sun will come back. Fall is here, but the summer will return. Rejoice. Rejoice."

SEPTEMBER 14 ❧ BE HAPPY NOW

No one can order up happiness for a friend, although often I would like to do so. We must not feel responsible for another's happiness, or they might notice and pretend to be content when they need to be able to talk about their sorrow.

I try not to say, be happy now, because no one can produce happiness on demand. It has to sneak in quietly, unnoticed and unobserved, like the late student in the classroom who will nonetheless say something brilliant later on.

But I can say count your blessings. I can be grateful for mercies large and small. I can look for beauty and exult in it. Because all those things could disappear and I will only notice I was happy in retrospect.

SEPTEMBER 15 ❧ LISTENING TO THE CHOIR

I know of few other places but church where this happens: a group of people gets together and practices, and then sings for us, unpaid, for the pleasure of it and to inspire our faith.

Philosopher Søren Kierkegaard argued that the audience in church is not those of us who sit in the pews but God, and I went along with that for many years. But now I am re-thinking my position. Our congregation has taken to applauding enthusiastically after the choir sings, and I am sure it is not because they have decided to be God. I think they are expressing gratitude.

Thank you for working at making beauty. Thank you for the pleasure you take in it.

Thank you. My faith lives in happy collaboration with my doubt. Thank you for supporting my belief.

SEPTEMBER 16 ❧ THE GODDESS

When my husband appeared robed in white ready to celebrate the outdoor wedding of our dear friend, the seven-year-old flower girl looked at him in astonishment. "You," she said in wonder, "look like a goddess."

Perhaps we grow more androgynous as we age. The psychologist Carl Jung thought so. I would like to think we simply live in a better time, when God can be feminine and a perceptive young girl can call a male Christian clergyperson a goddess, and the guy can delight in the compliment.

SEPTEMBER 17 ❧ HELP AT HAND

I am newly aware of the small and complicated universe that forms around a deathbed. All the relationships and issues of the outside world are here in miniature form. When a friend heard my mom was dying and appeared with generous offers of relief each day, I was inexplicably uneasy. I began to wonder if I was again the Bad Daughter, who could not watch through the night.

But who am I to declare what constitutes a proper deathwatch? The pastoral care department had provided a Bible, a selection of readings, quiet music. My friend, providing a source of animated conversation, was also offering a true holy moment, the assurance that life goes on. Her loving effort does not make mine less.

We get by with a little help from our friends. This too is holiness.

SEPTEMBER 18 ❧ THE WHITE COAT OF WISDOM

Elders have presence. The older they are the more they have. Which doesn't mean we have to be elders all the time, or ponderous *anytime*. "Elder" is a persona, a mask that we put on as we put on any other role.

When I was a reporter as well as a housewife, I learned to trust that my toilet-cleaning, soup-making self would gradually slip away on my way to the airport, so that I could arrive at my destination acting like the journalist I was. On the flight home, I would gradually pack away the journalist, remembering that I was, above all, Mom. In the same way, a doctor puts on his or her white coat, especially if she is your friend. Otherwise some invasive procedures might be embarrassing to you both.

Wearing an elder's presence like a robe can serve a shy person well. It makes it easier to get up and say wise things in public. The role of the elder entails drawing on his or her own inner wisdom. That is the white coat we put on.

And then we slip it off and play in the leaf piles with any children we can find.

SEPTEMBER 19 ❧ LAUGHTER

Not long before she died, my mother became mildly annoyed that all the people who were dancing in her room didn't have a good sense of rhythm. The day before, she had suggested that the staff was out of order, having a party and then leaving all those dirty pots and pans in her room for her to wash. She thought that her most recent visitor (a police officer) could fix them. My husband asked if he should bring his gun (I am afraid we both entered into this discussion vigourously).

She thought for a while and said "No. He doesn't need his gun." When Jim wondered about a squad car, she did think that would be good. This image – siren, car, unarmed cop rushing down the hallway – sent us into giggles that we tried to stifle.

But I think it was all right to laugh. Except for a brief spell in hospital some years before, when strong painkillers made her hallucinate for a day, my mother had always been extremely lucid. We knew that was her true self. This imposter would not be allowed to steal our memories. We would disarm her with laughter.

My mother laughed too.

SEPTEMBER 20 ❧ MOVIES

When we discovered that the last two movies based on Stieg Larsson's *Millennium Trilogy* were available, we immediately borrowed copies from the video store, ordered up a pizza, and settled on the couch.

They were the subtitled Swedish versions. We loved them, just the way I love Henning Mankell and Asa Larsson and Jo Nesbo and all the other Scandinavians who have a hammerlock on mystery writing these days.

Of course I enjoy the intricate plots, and the sympathy Larsson has for strong, unconventional women, the homicidal bullies (you really know who to dislike in these stories) and of course the satisfying endings.

But the real reason I love the films is that nobody is airbrushed into youthfulness. Lisbeth is usually too angry or blood-covered to be lovely. Mikael is a strictly middle-aged man – believably a journalist because nobody would consider his rumpled character a movie star – romantically entangled with his attractively wrinkled editor.

The demographics of the country are changing. The average age is rising. Expect more wrinkly movies. Being an elder might be fun.

SEPTEMBER 21 ⇌ INDIAN RESIDENTIAL SCHOOLS

The government and the four mainline Christian churches – Roman Catholic, Presbyterian, United, and Anglican – set out several generations ago to destroy First Nations culture in Canada.

They didn't hesitate to call it assimilation and they thought it was a good thing. They set up Indian Residential Schools – no term like First Nation would have been admitted at the time – and prevented, sometimes brutally, young children from speaking their own language.

They destroyed spirituality and family life, language and song. Many of the dances were lost, and precious artifacts were stolen and sold into private collections. The effects linger in a terrible legacy of damaged generations.

But as the stories began to come out, hearts were opened. People who had never known about the schools – white people – listened with tears running down their cheeks while First Nations elders talked about childhood hunger and beatings and neglect.

Maybe those hearts have not opened far enough. Maybe it is too late. Maybe people are flooding away from the churches (where the notion of repentance is understood) too quickly to make a turn-around possible.

But we must try. All the elders must do our work of healing the history of our country. That is the elder work.

SEPTEMBER 22 ❧ ELDER PRESENCE

In our community, a new L'Arche home was opening. L'Arche is a remarkable institution in which able-bodied men and women live as family with seriously handicapped men and women. They all learn from each other, and share a deep spirituality that spills out around them. L'Arche was started by philosopher and humanitarian Jean Vanier.

All went well until some of their potential neighbours called a meeting to express their concerns about "these people" moving into a house on their street. Would it hurt the neighbourhood? Would their homes be devalued by having a group residence in their midst? Finally, one neighbour, an elderly man of (famously) few words, rose to his feet. "These are good people," he said, and sat down.

There was silence. Then the meeting adjourned. The L'Arche community moved in, and invited all their neighbours to tea. There were no more complaints.

That is elder presence.

SEPTEMBER 23 ❧ SUPER SPECIES

When the old-growth forest is damaged, I grieve. When the sturgeon that once was abundant in the lake is scarce, I grieve. Sometimes it feels that I have spent my whole life grieving for something pristine that I will never find again.

When humans have damaged habitat enough to make life impossible for certain species, other species move in. The coypu, for instance, is a large water rat; not as attractive as a beaver, but nicely furred. Imported as a pelt-bearing creature, it has invaded both wilderness and built-up areas, thriving in outrageous conditions. Some were found flourishing in dairy farm sewage lagoons that were planted with the water hyacinths (themselves invasive) that coypu find tasty. Unfortunately, predators such as cougars and jackals that might find coypu delicious, and thus keep their numbers in check, are generally reluctant to live near humans.

I struggle with all this. Feral pigs, Asian carp – the list of opportunistic and rightly feared survivors goes on. But maybe something good could come out of this. Maybe, as author Garry Hamilton says in *Super Species: The Creatures That Will Dominate the Planet*, we can see them as "nature's attempt to start over, to rebuild ecological relationships in places where ecosystems have been shattered by...overhunting, land clearing and pollution."

We don't have a lot of time. But – as a super species that has learned to dominate the planet – we might clean up our messes before it is too late.

SEPTEMBER 24 ❧ OLD TRUTHS

Aging is hard because so many things we thought were permanent are revealed as transitory and trendy. What we thought was a terrific form of personality theory, for instance, now looks a bit grey and tired. What we thought was reasonable theology becomes questionable as we look at the consequences of literal biblical interpretation. We are left to figure out what we believe in the light of new knowledge.

Fortunately we are elders, and we have a long, long view to do that with.

I wonder if that is why sometimes some groups and institutions seem conflicted and cranky. Maybe it is all this hard work of throwing out and re-creating systems of belief.

SEPTEMBER 25 ❧ RUNNING OUT OF WATER

The Israelites are travelling from place to place in the desert, as the Lord had commanded, and they camp at Rephidim. There is no water. So they become annoyed with Moses for his bad leadership, and begin to hector him. (Based on Exodus 17:1–7)

Moses seems to me to be the quintessential elder for our day, caught in the role of leader in a tough situation. It seems unfair. If God is God, and all-powerful, why didn't God just serve up a supply of water whenever the people made camp?

In fact, why did God send them on this extended hiking trip in the first place? Whatever was God thinking?

I like to be in the bush. When I get home after camping, I feel that I am a competent person. We found our way (there are no road signs out on a lake), and we collected firewood, and hauled water, and I was strong.

Maybe God wished to instill a similar sense of competence in a people who – after all – had been slaves for generations. If everything they needed simply appeared, there would be no need for civic engagement, of passing judgment that Moses clearly had failed to govern properly.

So a highly symbolic ceremony followed, with the elders at the front. Moses' famous staff that had earlier parted the Red Sea smashed down on bare rock and produced a gush of water. God might be saying, remember, I parted the waters for you.

Humans are notoriously lax about civic engagement when their bellies are full. We might take this story to heart in a country where just over half of the population voted in the last federal election.

SEPTEMBER 26 ❧ ELDER WORK AGAIN

I have a small closet by today's standards. It's an old house. In the early 1900s I suppose people did not have wardrobes as large as we do today. In fact, while condo-shopping with one of my children, I was startled to see the large area now devoted to closets even as space becomes more costly.

As a young woman, without cash to spare, I made many of my clothes. But soon, as clothes became cheaper, I stopped making my own. Manufacturing moved to low-wage countries and garment-workers' unions in this country were weakened and tamed.

As an elder I remember when unions had strength and workers earned a living wage. There didn't seem to be so many people working at two jobs in order to survive. The top one hundred chief executive officers in Canada didn't have earnings 155 times higher than the average worker, and the gap between rich and poor wasn't growing every year.

Clothing cost more in those days. A small closet would suffice. People won't like to hear elders talk about that. But maybe we should.

SEPTEMBER 27 ❧ HAPPINESS

Sometimes Jim and I lie in bed and picture an imaginary whiteboard on the opposite wall. Each child is listed; we check off their status in terms of their well-being. When everyone is okay, we sigh happily and go to sleep.

"We are only as happy as our saddest child," the saying goes. I would like to take this burden off my children's shoulders. It is hard to be sad and have the added burden of knowing that, dammit, you are making your parents sad as well, thereby incurring the wrath of your siblings on top of all your other burdens.

Furthermore I know, as a modern woman, that I should not make my own happiness dependent on anyone else's. My feminist credentials are excellent.

But try as I might to be otherwise, I am unhappy if any child of mine is sad. And I'd like to point out that – according to the biblical narrative – God feels the same way. The shepherd goes off to find the missing sheep, leaving the others to fend for themselves. The father waits anxiously for his prodigal son, even though the stay-at-home one is serving him faithfully.

There's nothing else for it. God is a mother (or father). We knew that all along.

SEPTEMBER 28 ✤ BEAUTY AND UGLINESS

Design guru Bruce Mau was asked to deliver a lecture in Sudbury, Ontario, where he had grown up. He accompanied his talk with images, including, in his words, "four typical Sudbury street corners. Cold and grey, harsh and desolate."

Indeed. I also live in a northern Ontario town, and we can do desolate as well as anyone.

But Mau is an internationally famous designer. He led his audience through a strategy to create "a park with a city in it," instead of a grey city enlivened with a few patches of green. Soon after that, *Imagine Sudbury* was born, a group determined to develop exactly what he had proposed – a park, with a city in it.

"Beauty doesn't cost more than ugly," Mau had told them. I'm going to rehearse that, gratefully, for every civic meeting I attend.

Beauty doesn't cost more than ugly.

SEPTEMBER 29 ❧ SWEETMAN'S GARDEN: FIGHTING FOR BEAUTY

When city council offered a plan to build houses on a beautiful old garden, citizens rallied and saved the garden. Or so we thought. Suddenly one morning we opened our paper to discover that a hydro substation was planned for the garden.

It was a complete triumph of ugly over beautiful.

The Friends of Sweetman's Garden swung into action again. We walked for hours, leafleting neighbourhoods again, alerting green-lovers to a public hearing on the matter. Media releases were written, a quiet walk in the garden was undertaken with the new CEO of the hydro company.

We were already exhausted. This seemed to be one more blow. We wondered about giving up. And then came the night of a public hearing in the council chambers.

The chambers were packed. One person after another rose to speak passionately and eloquently on behalf of beauty. Oh, they may have been referring to the garden and how they loved it, but they were talking about the sheer impact of any form of natural beauty on the lives of every human being. A doctor described beauty passionately in terms of health, gardeners described it in terms of a wonderful collection of perennials and shade trees, and children – one of whom presented a framed photograph of the garden at its height to the hydro official – described it in terms of play.

The substation was built in an alternate, less historical, less obtrusive location.

Beauty can triumph over ugliness. Every body counts in the fight for it. Elders can pack seats in a public meeting even if they don't want to speak.

SEPTEMBER 30 ❧ AFTERLIFE

I don't know. People seem to think the question of an afterlife is a huge part of religion. It is not. I suspect, at death, my body becomes earth again, which is fine with me. Eventually, if or when Earth herself tumbles into a black hole, I will be stardust. I like that concept very much.

I do know that *this* is heaven, here, now. Even when I am worried about one child or another, one relative or friend or another, or my rickety neck. This is paradise now.

What comes after life is a mystery that will look after itself. I don't know for sure, but I think that "God" is not an old man with a long white beard, but a mystery in Herself.

OCTOBER 1 ❧ RELINQUISHMENT

Have you thought about relinquishment?" Jim said, brandishing a book by theologian Walter Brueggemann, whom we both admire. Not much. But I know Jim has, so I studied the passage carefully. It is about giving up power and glory. "This is a question for men," I said, "not women." We talked for a while about my issues with power. Women – at least, of my age – cannot be concerned with the relinquishment of power. Even after feminism has been articulated so wonderfully, by so many brilliant women, we are less in need of letting go of our authority than of picking it up. Brueggeman's argument is lovely, but it is a male one. Outside my window the maple tree shrugs leaves until a vast red carpet is spread on the ground. Unharvested fruit drops intermittently from the crabapple, and the foliage-heavy garden is lit only by a few foxgloves that have mistaken the season and decided to bloom. It is the season of relinquishment. Everything is in its time. Someday women, too, will note where they must surrender power. But first we need our summer in the sun.

OCTOBER 2 ❧ AUTUMN

My great tree trembles outside the glass
Closed now in the chill.

Flowers struggle on, doomed.

Clouds pile strangely above silent streets.
Rain falls.

Pumpkins hasten to fatten,
Beans flourish and lengthen

Tomatoes redden
 As the garden slows and yellows

And the firewood arrives
And the ferns are lifted up
  to dot the house inside,
    small deposits against endless white and rain.

The silent goddess trembles for her child who moves below.
We burrow into blessed winter,
one more rest before the long dark.

OCTOBER 3 ❧ NON-EXPERTS

I am not an expert in any healing art. I am just a friend, and often a terribly absent-minded one. Once I appeared at a friend's door with a birthday cake, lit with candles, daughter by my side. A good gesture, but it was not her birthday. She was in the middle of a delicate meeting, so we couldn't even go in to celebrate her non-birthday. I believe they enjoyed the cake at the meeting though.

Still, sometimes people do me the honour of sending me their dreams, because I have studied my own for many years, and have read quite a bit about them. This does not guarantee that I will be able to understand what they are about. But the dreams arrive anyway, by email and snail mail and fax. Sometimes people phone. Sometimes I open the front door and they are in my mailbox, delivered (I presume) early in the morning after a dream-filled night.

I sink humbly into these dreams. It is much easier to live into someone else's dream instead of my own, to call up everything I know about the friend who has entrusted it to me. I have no stake in suppressing anything that wants to be brought to light. That is quite unlike my own dreams, in which my own psyche campaigns against the release of the "shadow" contents the dream reveals.

So I immerse myself in my friend's dream. When it has told me all that I can hear, I offer it back to the one who sent it. It is always sent with the proviso that the dream belongs only to the dreamer. He or she is in charge of the interpretation.

Sometimes in this process I unexpectedly learn a great deal about a dream of my own. Perhaps the other's dream helps me bypass my own vigilance against difficult learnings about my own self. Sometimes I just enjoy a deepened friendship.

It is not always necessary to be an expert to serve a friend.

OCTOBER 4 ❧ SAINT FRANCIS

This is the feast day of Saint Francis. We have a little statue of him in the garden. Eli is taller than Saint Francis now, although there was a time when they stood eye to eye.

I am very fond of the patron saint of the environment and animals. His figure is graced by a deer nestled in the saint's stony arms, and a couple of birds sit on his shoulder.

The winter that he and Saint Francis first met, Eli suggested that the saint might be cold, so we wrapped a blanket around him, and it stayed there all that winter. I don't know if it warmed Saint Francis. It warmed my heart.

Eli was born in San Francisco, the city of Saint Francis.

In summer the goat's beard and astilbe, which have become mixed together, are lovely gathered around St. Francis' head and shoulders. Later a tall daylily, one of the late bloomers, stands beside him like a trumpet-bearing sentry.

My father grew goat's beard and astilbe. His name was Frank.
A few friends called him Francis.

My father fed the birds.

OCTOBER 5 ❧ SINGLE ELDER WOMEN

I have a friend who is a single mother. I have known her for thirty years. She has raised a fine son, and created a rare garden, and served her profession very well into her semi-retirement.

This was not easy. I could see that, from the outside. But she did not complain. She asked for help from her friends when she needed it, and provided help to all of us when we needed it. Her ability to seek help – even though she is in one of the "helping" professions herself – has been a marvellous model for all of us who like to think of ourselves as rescuers. It made it easy to go to her for help when our turns came to be rescued.

Many elders are single women. Those who are not yet, may be so one day. Learning to ask friends for help is a great gift to them. Then they can see how it is done.

OCTOBER 6 ❧ SINGLE ELDER WOMEN (TWO)

One single woman friend, now an elder, has been strengthening her circles of friendship for many years. The ties she has created are magnificent. Every Sunday night, a group of friends, married and not, gather at her house, and she cooks dinner for them. She loves to cook.

So they are tightly bonded to her and to each other. They care for one another in sickness, they rejoice in each other's triumphs. No new grandchild, no wedding, no graduation goes uncelebrated. They are family in a way that many families never quite manage, friends in a way that restores one's faith in humanity.

Also, dinner is extremely good. There are ways to be single, and an elder, and dearly, dearly loved. We need to practice these skills long before we are old so we will be ready.

OCTOBER 7 ❧ THE OCCUPIERS

One task suited to the expertise of elders is making sure that the correct names for roles and people are retained. Many such terms are rapidly being destroyed. Retired University of Toronto physicist Ursula Franklin argues that the new, substitute names are being offered by what she refers to as "an army of marketeers...who run the country for the benefit of the occupier."

The goal of the occupiers is privatization, which, in its most brutal terms, means to provide investment and profit opportunities in all those areas that people previously had set aside as common holdings – culture, health care, education, publishing, housing, nature, sports, prisons. Once dismantled, the "public sphere" can be more easily "occupied" – turned over to what I call the Empire of the Marketeers. These warlords will convert the ill-health and misery and basic needs of our neighbours into investment opportunities for the next round of global capitalism.[5]

Although this occupying power does not wear a uniform, says Franklin, members can be identified by their language, which converts real people and real experiences into abstract generalities. By consciously avoiding their language, elders can lead the way in refusing to be absorbed into the marketeer mindset.

Instead of saying "providers and users of health care," for instance, we might offer the old-fashioned terms "doctors and nurses and patients." Instead of "consumers of education" we might use "teachers and students." Members of our "friends, families, and communities" are not merely "taxpayers" or "stakeholders."

That last term, stakeholders, always makes me think of an army of righteous citizens ready to do war on vampires. When the body politic is subject to bloodletting, this might be an appropriate image.

OCTOBER 8 ❧ MANAGING POLITICIANS

Remember the Hebrew concept of *tsimtsum*. God once did many miracles, but it became time for humans to grow up. So God moved aside a little (*tsimtsum*) in order to give us room to mature.

We have the right, then, and the authority, to insist that those who serve us as leaders behave as grownups.

I am writing this at a time when behaviour in the Canadian House of Commons reminds me of certain frat parties I attended as a student. Some of the participants seem drunk with power, raucous, bullying. At the same time, instead of speaking for themselves, they toe a party line, loudly repeating the slogan of the day over and over.

This is not adult behaviour. We cannot heal the world or our country until we, as elders, demand maturity from those we have elected to serve us. Citizens fortunate enough to be represented by a person of dignity and compassion could find ways to express their gratitude to him or her. Those who are saddled with the permanently immature could let them know their time in politics is limited, and why.

OCTOBER 9 ❧ FICTIONAL GRIEF

This is ridiculous. One of my favourite mystery writers has just killed off his main character. So I am mourning a fictitious character. As if the world did not contain enough real suffering and death, I have to get all teary about a figment of someone's imagination.

I feel just like the little girl in the Robert Munsch story *Put Me in a Book*. She ended up in a book and couldn't get out. I sought out the mystery author's web site, parsing the phrasing of the blurb for his next novel. Hmm. The character I cherish is "gone," in the words of the description. Well, maybe he didn't die and has just "gone" for a rest somewhere.

Until I find myself reading about his funeral in the next book, I will have hope. But this is ridiculous. I have hope for life in a person who never existed in the first place.

An atheist might say religion is a little like that. It is ridiculous, no doubt. But narrative – the Bible and my mystery novel are both narratives – has the power to illuminate our lives. It can translate the disharmony and chaos of our world into a language of justice, even love.

That is not ridiculous at all.

OCTOBER 10 ❧ ANGELS

Angels exist. When my mother was dying, for months my friends came and sat with her, day after day, feeding her and talking to her. The latter was no mean feat, because they had to lean way over her bed and shout in her ear.

One day we were convinced she was close to the end. Then our friend Wanda came in, chatted at leisure, held her hand, and got up to go. My mother rang out, "Thank you, Wanda" at the top of her seriously compromised lungs.

We had no idea she could make a sound, much less words.

It is only later that I recognize my friends as angels. Not just as kind persons, which they are, but holy kind persons, letting a miracle float through them that brings about the power of speech.

OCTOBER 11 ❧ GOD

It's hard to pin down a definition of God. Orthodox Jews acknowledge this impossibility and the hubris of such an attempt by spelling it G-d.

I think I sometimes hear from God, even if I have trouble explaining who and what exactly God is. When a flat, firm statement appears in my dream, I believe it comes either from some extremely wise part of me, or from God.

"You can't focus two things at the same time." I heard that the other day in a dream. What's a confirmed multi-tasker to do then? The Bible pronounces on this as well: "You cannot serve two masters...You cannot serve both God and Mammon."

That doesn't necessarily mean it is the voice of God. The Bible was written by people, after all. But maybe they had dreams, like mine, and just wrote down what they heard.

Maybe the *dreams* came from God.

OCTOBER 12 ❧ ANAM CARA

For several years I bartered dream sessions for yoga lessons with a friend. She is highly skilled in both disciplines. She would arrive once every two weeks with strong arguments for my not missing yoga class, along with her dreams, which were already thoughtfully analyzed.

I would try to add something. Sometimes I could. An outsider can usually produce some insight that the dreamer can't see, simply because the issue is jammed so fiercely into our unconscious that we just can't get at it.

Still, I wasn't always useful. Her knowledge of the art of dream work was much deeper than my own.

But when she was getting ready to move away, she explained how grateful she was for our time together. It was, she said, because of the unconditional acceptance I always offered. That gave her the courage to delve into her own "shadow," as we call the most elusive area of our unconscious, and release what was absorbing so much of her energy.

It's a worthy job for anyone, that journey into our soul and back. It's too hard to undertake at any depth on our own, though. We need a friend to be an anchor, and to be unsurprised by whatever surfaces. Because each one of us – including the kind and compassionate among us, the looked-up-to who seem to have it all together – has a shadow filled with fearsome-seeming things. They shrivel when confronted, but it helps to have a companion.

The Celts called such a friend *anam cara*. Soul friend. When I salute the morning sun in yoga pose, I think of her.

OCTOBER 13 ❧ POWER

Elder women need to pick up their power when they have an opportunity to heal someone in pain; when instinct tells them they can be useful. When they recognize a schoolyard bully still present in a middle-aged adult's body. When the Earth who is our mother hurts. When the water is threatened.

We should not be discouraged by our lack of experience in using power, or the chance that we may cry. We can offer the clarity of vision that is often granted to people like ourselves, who have had a long life unobscured by too much power.

It is our responsibility as an elder.

OCTOBER 14 ❧ THE HEAD OF THE FAMILY

There's a trick to being a wise old elder. Know who you are, and simply operate out of that. Don't overwork at bringing about good outcomes; it just sets up resistance. Don't try to change a friend's course according to your own vision. Don't be overproductive. Be playful. Don't be anxious.

But be connected. Stay in touch with those you love. Have fun.

I break all these rules all the time. I am a conscientious, anxious, overproductive perfectionist (my family can tell you that) and all the more so with those very close to me.

I have spent a lifetime trying to unlearn this behaviour. In my attempts to be self-differentiated – not entangled – I study dreams, read books, talk to my very wise spouse, and think a lot. Oh, and write a lot, too. Readers may think I write books for them, and I do. But I also write because sometimes that moment I see the words is the first indication for me that I might know something useful.

Um, just offering some thoughts. No pressure.

OCTOBER 15 ❧ PRAYERS FOR THE DYING

Some dying people – even if they don't admit Death's presence kindly – will want you to pray with them. Many of us feel entirely inadequate to the task. But I agree with the Dutch priest Henri Nouwen, who said that we cannot leave the spiritual task of caring to specialists alone. "Every human being has a great, yet often unknown, gift to care."

People who are not doctors sometimes are a healing presence. People who are not teachers often teach important things. And people who have the courage to sit with the pain of someone they love make way for the presence of God.

OCTOBER 16 ❧ WAR

I was born during World War II. A bookish child, I read *The Rise and Fall of the Third Reich* when I was about twelve, and soon afterwards, *A Day in the Life of Ivan Denisovitch*. I can still see in my mind the rose-coloured cushions on the window-seat where I curled, reading, shocked. Later, I interviewed missionaries affected by the Korean War, and caught a glimpse of its power in the lives of that generation.

During the Viet Nam war, my spouse and I spent two years in the United States. The morning after four students were killed at Kent State University, I received a phone call from the minister of the church we were attending. He asked how he could move to Canada.

In occupied East Germany before the Berlin Wall came down, I walked with a German-born friend, who – very uncharacteristically – spat at the Russian embassy, enraged by his own memories.

These wars and more – Rwanda, Kosovo, Sudan, Iraq, Afghanistan, Central America – have taken place in my lifetime on the planet we all inhabit. I have met a few of those who endured famine and homelessness and survived with their humanity and grace intact.

I have never been hungry a day in my life.

We who have never been hungry have a duty to watch the news. As I write, revolution sweeps across the Arab world. We have a duty to sort through the convoluted politics that lie behind this.

As elders, we carry within us the memory of many wars even if we did not attend them. We have the long view. We need to study each conflict as it comes in order to talk intelligently about it with our friends and press our government to the action that will bring peace with justice.

OCTOBER 17 ❧ COURAGE

My mother did not die quietly. Once, after we thought she would go overnight, I found myself the next day writing to the grandchildren:

Grandma has once again defied the odds and is sitting up in bed, perfectly lucid and breathing quite well. I had called Uncle Larry last night, and it really looked as if they might want to come over. So they are now on their way. We informed Grandma that she would see them this afternoon and she was immediately alert. "WHY?" she wanted to know.

"It's a nice day for travelling..." is the best I could come up with.

So, although yesterday was a day when I discovered (ambushed by my own tears) that you are never ready for your parent to die, today I am reminded that Grandma is still a suspicious, canny Scot, and will set out to disprove any thought that her children should gather to bid her farewell. In her mind at least, she is not going yet.

I hope I will be as brave.

OCTOBER 18 ❧ GRANDCHILDREN IN SOLIDARITY

My e-letters to all my mother's grandchildren brought replies that gave us fresh energy. They celebrated her.

Memo From: Tracy

Subject: Grandma update

Well all be darned. grandma is one wild cookie and should get the scared-ya-didn't-I award.

mom, thanks for being so brave and keeping us all informed. hi uncle larry and aunt rhea and philip...maybe we should all have a glass of port in our respective homes in honour of grandma's sassy spirit...

I love you all. I'll be home by tonight.

OCTOBER 19 ❧ WRINKLES

I asked my spouse how he felt about wrinkles. On me, that is. I am not giving up my feminist principles. I wasn't asking if I should seek out botox injections, or some new miracle cream. I wasn't about to change the way I am. I just wondered.

He talked about the woman he had called his *mamacita* in El Salvador, her leathery face always full of joy despite her harsh circumstances. He talked about his admiration for June Callwood, and other older women who seem at peace with themselves.

He quite admires my wrinkles.

I am pleased to report this response. I am very pleased to be seen to be old when I have such company.

OCTOBER 20 ❧ FURTHERMORE

There's a certain advantage in being unabashedly old. In a youth culture, in which you are hardly expected to be able to produce coherent sentences past the age of sixty, it gives you the advantage of surprise. (She speaks!)

Also, I don't feel the need to dress up much anymore. (Some would say I never did.) It means I have cleaner, sparer closets, and more money to spend on other things, like snowshoes and books and lots of fresh fruit and vegetables every day.

And there's a subtle androgynous quality in my relationships. I don't have to negotiate my way through flirtation (fun though that is) and I don't have to treat a man's ego as if it was liable to shatter if I fail to hang on the guy's every word. (Okay, maybe I never did that much either, but I was born in the early 1940s, and some things don't go away easily.) We can treat each other with equal dignity and respect.

Freedom for women is more than just having the vote.

OCTOBER 21 ❧ THE DYING

During my mother's dying, I began to understand how it was important to listen carefully and try to speak her language. Just because it was not always logical doesn't mean it didn't make sense.

The day she complained about (non-existent) dirty pots and cutlery under her bed, an alert staff member had a quick response. "It's all right," she said. "I have already put them in the dishwasher."

From many years of meals with my mother, I knew what was coming next.

"Oh, no!" she said. "Not the knives. They have wooden handles."

"I'll go right away and get those out," said the caregiver. My mother was immediately less agitated.

It was a good instance of us entering her world, not asking her to come to us. It required a sensitivity that I wish I had had in more abundance. Like the day I went to see her and she was terribly worried about "the kid out in the rain" who turned out to be me, at five "with no clothes on." I immediately said that I was here, dry and fully clothed, and we both laughed.

It was not a bad response. But I wish now that I had said "I know you were a good mother to that little girl. I know you would never have left her out in the rain."

Or maybe I could have said, "We have always loved the wonderful way you care for us."

I was so wrapped up in her dying. But my mother's dying took a long time. Now, at a distance, I think that was because she was worried she had not done her job well.

If we are vigilant, we might create contentment.

OCTOBER 22 ❧ CONFIDENCE

I have had the good fortune to be married to a guy who likes to give away his white male power. He is pleased to slide into the background when there is a chance for someone else to have the spotlight, particularly if that someone is often overlooked. A person living in poverty, for example, or a layperson in an ecclesiastical setting, a member of a minority group in the midst of the dominant culture.

He admires women. I attribute this to his mother, who was an admirable woman.

It's a little too late to wonder, but I do anyway. Would I have written books (it's harder to do this than you might think) without his firm belief that I was capable of it?

Many writers can write only because they are able to ignore the demon on their shoulder – at least that's where mine sits, close to my right ear – whispering, "This is no good. This is stupid, really worthless stuff." I have learned to slap that demon down partly because I have a large, firm, spousal presence who bounces down the stairs after reading something I wrote twenty years ago saying, "Wow, this is still good!"

Memo to elder women. Tell your daughters and granddaughters, if they decide to marry, to choose a person who admires and likes women.

Our daughters will succeed anyway. But this makes it much easier.

OCTOBER 23 ❧ AUTHORITY

What gives elders the right to hold forth on anything, even though they have, in my friend Christel's words, "the long view"? How do we know we are acting as elders, and not just cantankerous old women, when we write a letter to the editor?

Perhaps time has something to do with it. We have time to read the papers and listen to the speeches and think about what we have read and heard. We can consider when we last heard certain arguments, and how that worked out.

This does not let us off the hook in terms of figuring out the right way ahead. Viet Nam happened. So did Rwanda. Each one of us has this difficult task of sorting out falsehood from truth, of delineating a true and prophetic vision for our community and country ourselves. That is our work as elders.

Our first job is to seek the truth, and then to lead our own lives in its light.

And just for the record, there's nothing wrong with being a cantankerous old woman.

OCTOBER 24 ❧ LOVE

A long marriage (I cannot speak for any other, now) teaches us a great deal about love. If you marry young, as we did, the little dance of intimacy is sure-footed. It is easy to share identities when you are young.

But love is a dance. You move close and then step back, close and then back. Even those who marry young shift a little apart at times, impelled by the need to preserve one's own self. Shared identity is sweet, and independent thought is priceless.

If you marry later, already accustomed to being your own person, this lust for individual thought may be easier to bear, I don't know.

But now I am an elder. It is to sigh with relief. When either of us becomes intrusive – "You could write 'Welcome to your new house!'" advised Jim helpfully the other day, when I was signing a book for someone – we just laugh. (He had the grace to look sheepish. I have signed thousands of books.)

Similarly, when I begin to tell him what he already knows very well – that the present government is dismantling everything of value and will ruin – ruin – the country, he looks at me as if this was a fresh, rare insight on my part, and nods vigourously.

Neither of us can die before the other. It would take too long to train a new spouse to this perfection.

OCTOBER 25 ❧ LINGER LUNCH

After Sunday worship, in our congregation, we have lunch. We have done this for more than thirty years. For some elderly singles, it means a regular, anticipated, social time with people they like of every generation. It is a time to sing happy birthday, a time to say goodbye if someone is moving away, a time to celebrate anniversaries of any kind. Meetings are sometimes squeezed in around a table.

We also have downtown neighbours who regularly join us, people who are not formally members of the congregation, who do not attend worship, who live in straitened circumstances or perhaps on the street.

Our congregation contains a number of saints. I know no other word to describe those who are determined that the hungry will be properly fed, with hot turkey soup or chili or a casserole and something green, even if it just celery, and dessert. Always dessert, because their lives are hard and this is something to look forward to.

This is not easy for everyone. I find myself racing to sit with someone I just saw at worship. I need to visit with so-and-so, I rationalize. She is sitting alone.

But there are others, braver, who sit with the homeless and chat, and make them feel at home here. Some then feel welcome enough to make their way to the kitchen and help with the cleanup.

This is a costly form of justice-seeking. If one has money, it is not hard to give it. If one is used to making speeches, it is not hard to lobby governments for the improved services we desperately need. It is much harder to sit down with someone who might look, or possibly smell, grungy and who finds small talk utterly beyond them.

Oh, I know we are all saints, all who attend here for worship or for lunch. We are all God's people, rich, and middle-class, and impoverished. Some of us, from both groups, know how to erase the boundaries between us. And I am watching and learning from them, because I cannot let others carry my compassion for me forever.

OCTOBER 26 ❧ HEALING FRIENDS

Most forms of therapy don't involve the therapist sharing much about his or her own life. It crosses professional boundaries. It's a very good rule. But it leaves, then, a space for friendship with someone who is not the therapist, someone who also has wounds and harsh memories. You and they can be less lonely, and that is very healing.

But handle this with care. If you are the one in anguish, don't try to make one friend carry it all. Dependency (and we are all allowed to be dependent sometimes) needs to be distributed carefully.

On the other hand, if you are the one depended upon, and it becomes too draining, spread the dependency. Call on other friends. Consider the safety spiel on airplanes: put your own oxygen mask on first, and then adjust your friend's. You can help no one if you are gasping for breath.

If someone has made a point of telling you this already, they may have noticed something. You may need to take a close look at your relationships. Someone may be sucking all the air out of your life, and that's not healing for either of you.

Send that someone back to his or her therapist.

OCTOBER 27 ❧ LOYALTIES

We have a new traffic island downtown, very expensive, lots of brick and clever antique-looking light standards. The designers included lots of trees, and so they win my approval.

But there have been rumblings from some citizens, unhappy about their taxes, who wonder why city council approved millions of dollars on this one short stretch of roadway.

"But we didn't spend *your* tax money," is the reply. "Most of it came from federal grants."

This leads me to believe that our loyalties as citizens have become too narrow. I pay federal taxes as well. It is still my money. And I like my city to look good, and I like traffic improvements at that corner, so I am not complaining, not at all.

But how did we come to believe that citizenship in a city removes us from citizenship in a nation? And citizenship in a nation does not excuse us from being a member of the global village. Our world view should not become so narrow that we forget the claims laid on our hearts by nations struggling with drought and war and famine.

Who are my people? It's a good question to ponder for a day.

OCTOBER 28 ❧ RELINQUISHMENT AND MYSTICISM

In our house, we peruse two different newspapers in the morning, reading bits aloud. (Did I mention that being an elder is a good life?) Then we compose letters to the editors, and often even send them. Judging by the current polls, the sweep of right-wing thinking seems inexorable. It is mystifying to us, especially given the way our two papers lay out the brutal facts morning after morning: this parliamentary process held in contempt, this piece of information unforthcoming, this civil servant bullied and shamed. We rant at each other about these things as if we were not already in perfect accord. Democracy in this country is going downhill fast. We are in despair.

Of course, that gives us something to relinquish: our sadness and despair.

Relinquishment is the way of the mystics.

The mystical experience, said theologian Dorothee Soelle, involves a yielding up of the self. "We have to strip ourselves of the images we have lived by and leave our egos behind. On its deepest level, we have to put our own sadness, our own depression, behind us."

Well, yes, I have become attached to my morning rant. Along with two cups of strong coffee, it gets the blood going. This sadness is my own. I have made it so, and I cling to it.

But I can walk the labyrinth, or pray, or meditate upon scripture, dissolving my self in God, leaving my argumentative self-righteousness behind.

At Sunday worship our choir sings the words of the mystic Julian of Norwich. "All will be well again." I listen and sigh gently, abandoning my precious despair.

OCTOBER 29 ❧ NEW SYSTEMS OF MEANING

We can find hope, says theologian Douglas John Hall, if we face our despair, and seek out new avenues of meaning now that the old ones – the old Empire of Christendom, the old way of treating Creation as a resource to be plundered – are no longer valid. "Only a new system of meaning," he says, "can provide the permission that the repressed despair needs if it is to name and replace bogus goals and cheap hopes."

But creating a new system of meaning is a big order. The complete works of systematic theologian Karl Barth, who was very good at this, are tucked in my husband's closet under his shoes, all thirteen heavy hardcover texts complete with dust jackets. We don't use them. We don't have space for them. But we aren't quite sure we can get rid of them.

And then I watch the young families who arrive at our church for a Transition Town meeting or a seed exchange, full of joy. They are the ones we leave to handle a sullied Creation, and they are full of hope that they can do it. Clearly, in the effort to reclaim a farm economy for local people and find clean sources of power and rebuild ties among people of good will, they are making a brave new system of meaning.

They have left despair behind. It gives me hope.

OCTOBER 30 ❧ THE KINGDOM OF GOD

You are not far from the Kingdom of God. It is a phrase I have been pondering for a long time; and it keeps grabbing me, demanding that I figure out what it means. Perhaps the Kingdom of God (or the Peaceable Kingdom or the Household of God) is the Truth and Reconciliation Commission in South Africa, or the commission of the same name on the Indian Residential Schools in Canada.

But then, where does that leave the long-held idea of Heaven as the Kingdom of God, the place where there is no more sorrow and angels flit about on compassionate missions? I mostly sidestep the question. But I wonder.

"You are not far from the Kingdom of God," said Jesus, meeting with teachers of the law. Perhaps he meant that *he* was the Kingdom of God. Perhaps humans can be the Kingdom of God.

My friend Bunty sent me an email. She wants me to call our member of Parliament and express my pleasure that he intends to vote for Bill C393, allowing cheap Canadian anti-retrovirals to go to Africa. She's also looking for "lots of bakers, a few more door people, a few models, and lots of kitchen help" for an up-coming fashion show.

Bunty is a member of the Grandmothers to Grandmothers campaign. A whole group of elder women in my city, along with 239 groups in other Canadian towns and cities, has sent over $10 million to help impoverished African grandmothers raise their grandchildren. The children's parents have died of AIDS. Grandmothers here hold bake sales and fashion shows and concerts to assist grandmothers there with housing grants and food and school fees for their grandchildren.

Perhaps elder women are the Kingdom of God.

OCTOBER 31 ❧ PRAYER FOR OCTOBER

God of little children wearing masks
Remind me of the masks I wear each day.
Help me know that I am not my costume, not my role.

God of little children dressed as ghosts
Remind me of the Holy Ghost you are.
Help me know your Spirit as my guide.

God of the small costumed child, witch, devil, vampire, cowboy,
princess...
Teach me to fear no thing within my soul.
Help me bring all darkness into light.

I am your faithful pagan, Mother-Father God,
Your faithful child who loves your sacred Earth.
I trust in you.
Amen.

NOVEMBER 1 ❧ SAMHAIN

This is New Year's Day for Celts, the beginning of the long sleep of winter, and a day for honouring the dead. The veil between the worlds is thin at the turning of the year.

This threshold time makes it a good night for dreaming, a good night for praying for a clean heart. "Let me not from the sight of thine eye," are the brave words found in one Celtic New Year's prayer.

It's a good night to ask for blessings. Your grandmother may be listening.

NOVEMBER 2 ❧ FIRE

We are separated from the other animals by our ability to create fire. No other creature can control it, and sometimes we can't. Dogs have chosen to join us in our comfort with fire, giving up their freedom in order to sleep on the hearth.

When I was little, my mother cooked on a wood stove in the kitchen. The fireplace in our living room was the other source of warmth. I remember this. Later, we moved to a more conventional house with an electric stove. But we still had a fireplace where we made popcorn in a blackened, lidded wire basket, shaking it back and forth over the coals.

Now, in my elder years, I laze by the fire in the evenings, like an old dog beloved enough to be allowed on the couch. I read my book. My husband feeds the fire, lovingly watched – I have no doubt of this – by ten thousand years of ancestors.

I am content.

NOVEMBER 3 ❧ CHURCH IMAGES

The church building where I attend is full of symbols, especially those that show our love of Creation. A stained glass window in the chapel is full of lakes and trees, deer and bear, while the antique windows in the sanctuary are replete with lilies. Stylized bellflowers are carved into the old oak pews.

On the Communion table are the dishes for bread and wine, because we serve the bread-God Jesus, the one who said to us, "Feed my sheep." I think he meant that in a literal as well as a symbolic sense. So when we serve the bread of Communion, it symbolizes our efforts to feed the world: the food bank, the Sunday lunch that welcomes all, including those with little income; the potluck suppers (any excuse).

We cannot literally feed the whole world. But we can model what it is to feed the world, and demand our politicians do this too. Joseph challenged Pharaoh in this way long ago. "You must feed your people," he said, risking execution. Our danger is not so great.

The most sacred symbol in our multi-symbol building is the bread. And the most sacred space is the kitchen.

NOVEMBER 4 ❧ PANCAKES

These pancakes are quick and good, and the recipe may be multiplied for a church lunch. They are so easy I don't wait for company to make them at home.

1 cup whole wheat flour
1 teaspoon baking powder
1 tablespoon butter or canola oil
1 egg
1 cup buttermilk

Mix flour and baking powder in a bowl. Melt butter in frying pan over medium heat. Add egg, melted butter, and buttermilk to flour mixture. Mix just enough to blend. Drop into the medium-hot pan by large spoonfuls. Flip when bubbles start to form. Cook until done.

Serve whatever you like on top. We like almost any berries, or unsweetened applesauce, along with maple syrup.

NOVEMBER 5 ❧ ELDER SENTIMENTALISM

In Joanna Skibsrud's lovely novel *The Sentimentalists*, a grandfather begins to build his own barrier to hold back the floodwaters of a massive government project that will destroy his town – including, of course, his own home. His grandson helps him.

It is futile to stand in the way of the "greatest technological feat so far known to man." But grandfather and grandson lug gravel and move stones, shoring up their little backyard dam until it's time for their move to the new "government house" that will replace their soon-to-be-drowned one.

Grandfather refuses to go, even when his son and grandson do so, and even when they drive daily to the old site and plead with him. The flood rises, and finally the police go in a boat to collect him as the water "reached the uppermost step, wetting his shoes." Fortunately they have brought along his grandson, and as the old man steps at last into the boat, "he held Owen's shoulder in order to steady himself."

This is what elders do. They shore up the old ways with tiny dams, even when it makes no sense. They enlist the help of the young in this project, and the young quite often accept. They stand together in the way of progress, so that those who know best must remove them consciously and deliberately.

Elders do this so the story of what happened will remain. Someday someone will hear it and ask why.

NOVEMBER 6 ❧ WHAT MATTERS

Grandchildren offer us a unique doorway into our grown children's lives. As soon as his or her own child is born, your child will know what you know – that after this nothing will ever matter more to them than this person in their arms. Nothing. Other things will be important but will never matter more.

So now our daughters and sons are joined to us in this sisterhood or brotherhood of parenting. It is a powerful association. Most elders, though, intuitively understand that this is an entrance with a door that opens and shuts, and will not expect it to be open all the time. In a crisis or a celebration it swings wide. We need to respect that it may be gently closed at other times.

That's a good time to rest up for when we are needed.

NOVEMBER 7 ❧ SMOKE

My husband knows this: a good woodpile lets the air blow through to dry the split logs without mould formation. Removing chunks of wood from this well-shaped structure does not disturb the whole pile. Carrying it up from the woodshed to the fireplace is excellent exercise.

If the wood is sufficiently dry, it burns very hot and creates only a hint of smoke. The chimney won't be lined with creosote, risking a chimney fire, and our neighbours won't end up inhaling our particulate matter.

All this is important. Wood, properly managed, is a renewable resource. Trees want to grow and require no help from us. If we use wood for heat, there is no need to prop up dictators in other parts of the world in order to obtain fossil fuel to keep us warm.

NOVEMBER 8 ❧ FUEL

Oh, I know. The modern world can't run on wood. Picture an airplane dropping out of the sky because the woodbin was insufficiently filled before takeoff. Joke.

And that's fine. I love planes and cars and electric stoves where I can turn a dial and produce the exact temperature that will bake muffins in a predictable amount of time. Miracles. Who would want to spend a day out of every week on maintenance, simply chopping wood to feed the fires?

All the same, I am grateful beyond measure to have lived in a time when my grandson can jam a marshmallow onto a stick and toast it carefully over coals and mash it onto a graham cracker with a square of chocolate and grin at me in chocolate-smeared delight.

Remember this, I whisper to him silently. Remember ten thousand years of flame, and life in a dark forest, and slowly-tamed wild dogs choosing us and our light and warmth.

Remember. This fire is what makes us human, different from the other animals.

NOVEMBER 9 ❧ WATER

When our grandson comes to visit in the summer we set up the sprinkler for him to run through. He shouts with happiness. We go to the beach and he plays in the waves; on a windy day they roll in like thunder. After a rain, we walk in the puddles.

We will teach him to canoe and we will swim off rocky outcrops and watch the minnows scramble to be fed.

When we are in Montreal and it rains, we watch rivers of water stream down the gutters. We visit every fountain we can find in a city devoted to splashing water, and we walk to the harbour playground so he can climb the big toy ship.

We came from water, we are made mostly of water. Water is required for our life. And for our play.

NOVEMBER 10 ❧ AIR

When your grown children worry about energy costs, offer an elder's advice. Tell them how to stay cool without using air conditioning.

Plant a shade tree (maple, oak, even poplar) on the south side. Best done when the house is built, but never too late.

Plant vines. They provide shade too.

Open windows on all sides of the house to allow a crossbreeze. Electric fans may be helpful.

When the sun is hot on the windows, close the curtains. Open them in the evening and get those fans going.

Move slowly and drink lots of water.

Remember, your windows are open; if your neighbours make noise, you will hear it. And vice versa. Be kind.

Cultivate a community of urban tree-lovers. More trees, more shade. More shade, less heat. Persuade enough citizens to plant a front yard tree and every sidewalk will be a cool walkway, and your house will be cooler too.

In the winter, cherish the cool air in your house. Put on a sweater or two. When your guests shiver uncontrollably, turn up the heat.

NOVEMBER 11 ❧ HOMELESS

I have felt homeless – or rather, country-less – only once before in my life. It was at Oka, Quebec, when the non-Native municipality attempted to turn a pine grove, the common land of the Mohawk, into a golf course. A standoff involving police, army, and Mohawk ensued. In the end, the pines remained and I got my country back.

Now I feel homeless again. As I write, the party in power is attempting to re-form Canada. It doesn't look like the country for which my uncles fought World War II, nor the compassionate one their generation created after they came home.

I would prefer a country in which the integrity commissioner protects whistle-blowers. I would prefer to have a long form census, because that collects data that interested organizations can use to track poverty, health issues, or household work. I prefer a country where government and church coalitions can work together to tackle poverty here and overseas.

I would prefer election ads to be respectful, and debate in the House of Commons to be substantive, as befits the lifeblood of democracy. I would prefer prisons be focused on rehabilitation and justice to be aimed at restoring harmony to the community. I prefer that veterans receive excellent benefits, and their privacy respected.

I would like to see much of Canada's aid go to Africa, the poorest continent on earth, and I would like our country to have a seat at the UN Security Council.

But when I think of where to turn – now that I feel in danger of losing my country – I consider the First Nations of this land. They also had their country re-formed, into an image that was far harder and far less spiritual than their own. For 500 years they have resisted efforts to stamp out their culture. They have survived.

I am determined that my Canada can also resist and survive. I don't know where else I can go.

NOVEMBER 12 ❧ EARTH

I turn over the vegetable patch, putting the garden away for winter. Every spadeful wakens earthworms; sow bugs scurry, or rest in ignorance of my work, already quiet, legs tucked, asleep. Five hundred million bacteria live in a gram of this soil along with a million or more (many more) actinomycetes. How many are there on this shovel? How can I possibly lift such a zoo, such an overwhelming population of fungi and protozoa, nematodes and centipedes and ants all slowing in their chewing and absorbing and churning and digesting my garden?

I put down my shovel.

Next spring, they will all wake up. The munching will go on, presenting food to the plants I seed here. The sun will come, and the sweet rain. The beans and tomatoes and dill and basil will flourish.

Spring will be soon enough to turn over the garden. Winter is given us for rest.

NOVEMBER 13 ❧ WHAT IF?

What if is one of the most valuable phrases ever invented. Without it, no new alternative is born. What if people demanded that our parliamentarians be respectful, even gracious with each other? What if we outlawed political attack ads? What if every child had free music lessons, and what if a little wilderness area was mandated for every neighbourhood? What if we had downward-facing shielded city street lights so that we could still see the stars?

It could be our morning prayer. We could all look out our windows each day as soon as we got up and say, *"What if...?"*

NOVEMBER 14 ❧ BIKE LANES AND SIDEWALKS

Even if we are too old to cycle, elders can still agitate for good bike lanes. (Actually, when is "too old"? Maybe never. Many people will ride their bike until their heart stops.) Good bike lanes get people to work and shopping. These lanes are best if they are curbed, to prevent cars from straying into them.

Elders can also hold out for sidewalks. Sidewalks can get you to the city centre if you live close enough, or to the store if your suburb is elder-friendly and has discovered the merits of small shopping areas integrated into the residential areas.

We need to do this for two reasons. First, elders remember bicycles and how we got around on them as children, in the era before fear overcame parents and they began to drive their children everywhere. We can help overcome that present-day fear by suggesting firmly to city planners that bike lanes are a necessity.

Secondly, as elders, we are going to lose our cars. Our vision is going to go, or at least our depth perception. Our reflexes will slow. Gasoline prices will rise, and we are on fixed incomes. For the day we can no longer drive, a sidewalk shaded by trees and dotted on the side with the occasional bench will be helpful. Or a good bike lane.

Sorry to point out all this news about what's ahead. But the good life as an elder requires forward planning.

NOVEMBER 15 ❧ GENERATIONS: A PARABLE OF MISINTERPRETATION

An old woman woke up one morning with a big black block of iron on her chest. She tugged and tugged, but it would not be dislodged.

She went to her doctor. He gave her a glass of water and some orange pills, but the big block did not move one inch.

She went to her minister, who talked quietly to the big block. It seemed to stir a little but settled back into place.

She went to the health food store and bought probiotics, Rescue Remedy, and vitamin D. The big block remained, although her allergies got better.

The old woman's little granddaughter came to visit. "Grandma, why are you angry with me?" asked the child when she saw the block. "What did I do wrong?"

Immediately the old woman saw her own grandmother standing before her, with a terrible black block on her chest. She had never asked her grandmother about it, thinking it was one of her own blocks that she had forgotten to put into her toy box. She thought it was her fault.

The old woman replied, "You are the light of my life. I was sad, not mad. And never, never, never because of you."

And then the black block crumbled into tiny pieces and fell on the floor. The grandmother and granddaughter made a big batch of cookies and went for a picnic, giggling all the way.

A third giggle could be heard from time to time, an echo. It sounded just like the little girl's great-great-grandmother.

NOVEMBER 16 ❧ CONFLICT

I greatly dislike conflict. My friends used to remind me to breathe whenever there was any unrest in any group at which I was present. After a while I learned to remind myself, because it is important for a reporter to handle conflict. Now I can be present at pitched verbal battles. Sometimes I get a little pale, but I keep breathing.

The thing is, nothing valuable happens without some conflict. Whenever we embark on something new or change direction or rethink something, something old has to go. Conflict emerges – naturally – because someone is attached to what's being scrapped.

But families (or other communities) work through necessary conflict better with "holy manners." That's a phrase my friend

Marion Pardy uses. She got it from author Gil Rendle. It means listening carefully to one another. It means operating not entirely out of rules and regulations, nor out of complete and unbridled freedom, but out of deep-rooted values like compassion and generosity.

Holy manners require courage and kindness and careful breathing. Don't forget the breathing.

NOVEMBER 17 ✺ MY MOTHER: REFUSING SPIRITUAL CARE

I think it is important to honour a dying person's decision about how they will meet death. One of the first things I learned from my mother's dying was that not everyone will admit they have a spiritual need. A kindly nurse offered to read scripture to her, and my mother shouted "NO!" Similarly, my mother made no requests for pastoral care. She was happy with pastoral visitors who came to see her only as long as they never offered a religious reason for the visit.

This was in keeping with her long-standing position that she would never die. Twenty-five years before, she had told me about a dream: "Your father came with a big suitcase," she told me, "and I said, 'No, I'm not going now.'"

Even when it became clear that there would be no sudden cure for old age (she was 96) we continued to honour her absolute refusal to greet the angel of death politely. He might be coming for her, but his entry would not be made easy.

I admire greatly my mother's desire to wring every last drop of goodness from life. I will try to be as stubborn.

NOVEMBER 18 ❧ WALKING AWAY

Sometimes an elder (or anyone) has to walk away from a difficult situation. But it's hard to know exactly when to do that. Is it when your being kind has tipped over into being a doormat? Or when your efforts to listen carefully are lost in the general din? Or maybe it is when you can no longer sleep because of the dialogue proceeding in your head, night after night.

Certainly it's time to remove yourself if your health is beginning to suffer. You could first ask these questions of yourself:

Will this organization or committee or board continue without me? Should it?

Is this argument really about what is being stated? (Think about this.)

If not, what is this fight about? Power? Loneliness? A desire for inclusion? Jealousy?

Is there any way I can respond to this unstated problem?

What good could come from my staying?

What good could come from my leaving?

All this might lead to a decision. Meantime, remember:

Most battles, in a family or in a group, are not about what they seem to be about. You can fix the stated issue, but if the real one is not addressed, the problem will come back.

Nobody is indispensable.

No organization can mandate a life sentence except the criminal justice system.

Oh yes, most important. Anxiety (especially on the part of a well-respected elder figure) is like gasoline on a fire. Be the non-anxious presence.

NOVEMBER 19 ❧ A GOOD LEAVING

You may decide that it is time to leave a beloved committee or organization and allow something new to be born in you, and in it. This can be quite difficult.

Stay calm. Don't slam any doors, or offer parting advice in a loud voice (metaphorically or literally).

Don't blame. Someone may be at fault. It could even be you.

Allow for a farewell party. Be gracious.

Rest. Think. Refrain from jumping into a new responsibility until you have figured out what part of the problem was in you. (Maybe you tried desperately to persuade everyone of your point of view, instead of simply leading the way ahead. Or maybe your connection with each member of the group failed, someone was left out, and all this fuss was because someone just wanted to be noticed.)

Breathe. Conflict and endings are part of life. You can't have new beginnings without them.

NOVEMBER 20 ❧ PERSUADE OR LEAD?

Slowly I have begun to realize that the attempt to persuade sets up an automatic resistance. The more elaborate the effort to persuade, the more powerful the resistance. For instance, while I love to receive the gift of a book, if it is accompanied by an injunction like, "You should really read this!" I almost invariably don't read it.

Groups and communities function like that too. I think that's why the best preachers don't preach, really. They just elegantly lay out their thoughts, and let listeners draw their own conclusions.

Telling people the answer only works if the question has been asked.

NOVEMBER 21 ❧ EXTERMINISM

Dorothee Soelle was a young girl in Germany during World War II, a passionate peace activist during the nuclear arms race, and a brilliant feminist theologian.

And she loved Creation, God's Creation. "It is not just survival instinct that makes me protest and fight against the military machine," she said. "I am far more impelled by my unswerving love for creation..."

Soelle warned us against people who "conspire to undo" Creation – those who rape the earth, starve the poor, and contribute to the build-up of arms. Her credentials were very good. Her childhood was spent in a country that was bent on all of the above.

I consider the industries of Canada's oil sands, its toxic tailing lakes visible from space. And Canadian arms sales to the Middle East from 2007 to the end of 2009 (last available figures): $153 million. And the 3.4 million Canadians who live in poverty (2008).

Exterminism is the word Soelle used to describe the philosophy of making the rich richer by exhausting the earth's resources. A useful word. Against the *exterminists* are those others who consider Earth sacred, who try to keep her healthy.

There are more of us all the time.

NOVEMBER 22 ❧ KINDNESS

Love one another, Jesus said. We find this hard to do, maybe because love has become an entirely complicated word. During the Middle Ages, the courtly love tradition got in the way of simple, tender (maybe self-sacrificing) affection and has remained with us ever since. A quick dictionary search for love calls up "romantic affair" and "passionate desire," as well as "something eliciting enthusiasm."

I think a reasonable alternative, at least until we can distinguish one form of love from another, might be kindness. We seem lacking in kindness, as if it is a weakness. It is not. It is synonymous with compassion, "to suffer with," the highest value in every one of the world's religions. Kindness and compassion bring with them a gentleness that our highly competitive society often overlooks.

Many bad things are undone by kindness. Try being kind at your next meeting (even if it's just meeting a neighbour on the street). See what happens.

NOVEMBER 23 ❧ MY MOTHER – INDEPENDENCE

As a child, I remember struggling with my mother's seeming omniscience. She would tell me what she thought best for me – sometimes sharply – and I would rebel and do it my way. It turned out she was nearly always right, and I would have to backtrack and regroup. It wasn't until I moved away from home that I learned to trust my own decision-making powers.

For a long time after that I was reluctant to accept any wisdom from her. I think I feared my hard-won independence of thought would vanish.

But as my mother grew frail and began her slow decline in death's waiting room, I began to trust her exploration of this uncharted territory. Some day I will be in this same room, loosening the bonds of time and space, like her. I will need to know how it is done.

NOVEMBER 24 ❧ QUARTERING

When I think I am being too polite, I remember my dad teaching me to canoe. "Quarter the waves," he said, showing me the correct angle so that I was not fighting the wind but using it. There's no need to hit things hard head-on if you can figure out a way to accomplish the same end by coming at it gently.

Elders trying to bring about change can become as burnt out and exhausted as any other activist (even though we can sleep in more). Graciousness and politeness work much of the time. You can save your strength for the times it doesn't.

NOVEMBER 25 ❧ NOVEMBER PRAYER

Bless the dark, God of sleep and winter.
Bless the cold.

Bless my neighbours, Goddess of the city.
Bless my home.

Bless the coming snow, God of crystal shapes.
Bless the ice.

Bless our fires, and all who knit sweaters.
Bless pesky snowsuits, and all who zip them up.
Bless snowplows and snowshoes, snow banks and snow shovels,
Skis and toboggans and skates and snow people,
Hats and scarves and mitts and
Spring.
Amen.

NOVEMBER 26 ❧ EXPRESSIONS OF CARE

We have different ways of expressing our affection for others, Jim and me. I like to write notes. When I get around to it. Sometimes I have composed them so carefully in my head I forget I haven't sent them, and the non-recipient never knows how warmly I was thinking of them.

Jim on the other hand, likes to drop everything and pick up the phone, or simply present himself at the person's door/office/cubicle. He likes to talk in person.

I suppose it doesn't hurt to try the ways of others once in a while. When I actually talk to someone – in the grocery store, say, or at a party – I am shocked (shocked!) at how delightful it is to talk with an acquaintance face-to-face.

NOVEMBER 27 ❧ THERAPY

I am a fan of family therapy and systems therapy and psycho-therapy. Massage therapy. Cognitive behavioural therapy, whatever that is. The list could go on. I am delighted by these close and ardent studies of the art of healing.

But I think the universal therapy is kindness. It is the instinctive, unstudied, child-like, and vulnerable opening of one's heart. It is the epitome of hospitality, the setting aside of one's own agenda. It is what we expect in families and public life and religious communities. When it is missing, we are damaged.

Fortunately, when we take the risk of quieting our own crowding concerns and saying with genuine interest, "How are you?" and listening, and then going with that person to the inner place where they are sad or happy, to mourn or celebrate with them as the moment demands, we are healed for a time. And so are they.

NOVEMBER 28 ❧ CONFIDENCE

... so that you are not lacking in any spiritual gift as you wait for the revealing of our Lord Jesus Christ. (I Corinthians 1:7)

Sometimes I am shocked at my own confidence. What gives me the right to suggest that cities should be blessed with urban forests and bike lanes? There is always another side to the story, and isn't it a little outrageous to think that I have the direct line to the truth?

I can only trust the spiritual gifts promised to us in scripture, trust the instincts and prayers and wisdom of my religious community. God "will always strengthen you to the end," says Saint Paul. I hope so.

The same week that some members of our community were showing up at Council, asking our city to live respectfully in Creation, they also put on the turkey supper. That's what really gives me confidence.

Because they are about getting their hands into dishwater, and carving up turkeys, and serving lots of dinners, and maybe being pretty tired at the end of the day. Saint Paul himself would be impressed with a group of people who don't assume that "spiritual gifts" means the good fortune just rolls in.

Spiritual gifts and confidence are founded on practical effort.

NOVEMBER 29 ❧ DREAMS OF DRIVING (TWO)

Sociologist Sara Lawrence-Lightfoot describes in *The Third Chapter* how, at retirement, we may find it necessary to drift. Pause time, while we figure out what we want to do with the rest of our life. I dreamed this about a year after I retired.

I am trying to leave somewhere in a car. My friend Z is with me and I can't see where we are going, and am hunched over the wheel, peering. I am dimly aware of trees as I back up. We drive on a narrow road, almost a pathway, through the woods. Then

I make a false turn into an auto showroom of some kind, but hastily back down those steps and go on.

Then we are at a service station. Although she is female, Z is also male, which shows when she bustles around washing the car windows so I can see. At first I say nothing, but then some youths start to laugh. I decide I had better tell her that she is "untucked." She pulls herself together.

Dreams know how to get your attention. The image of Z (part of my own psyche) as a hermaphrodite is shocking. The dream seems to be saying, "Wake up!" It may also affirm the power of any woman elder who has lived long enough to integrate the emotional skills of the opposite sex.

I am wondering where I am going ("can't see", "backing up") and so make a false turn into something that is just for "show." (Car travel is often a metaphor for the way we are going through life. In this dream I am driving. When I am particularly out of control my brother, who is blind in real life, is at the wheel. He finds these dreams entertaining when I mention them.)

A life of some "service" is part of the way forward ("washing the car windows so I see"). But the dream suggests that I am still undone, inappropriate, untucked. It is time for me to "pull myself together."

And don't even consider a life that is all for "show."

NOVEMBER 30 ❧ LOVE REVISITED

Four-year-old Eli and his grandfather have a tradition. Whenever they see a full moon, they say, "I love you," to the other, even if they are hundreds of miles apart.

In the dark of early winter we were visiting Montreal. On our way from shopping, we were crossing six lanes of heavy traffic on boulevard René-Lévesque, clutching our groceries and our grandson's hands.

Suddenly he spotted the full moon. "I love you, Baba!" he shouted at the top of his lungs.

"I love you, Eli!" shouted Baba.

"We love each other!" Eli shouted to the moon and the rushing cars and the people walking home from work, tired, no doubt, and cold in the gathering winter.

Love may not always conquer all. But it sure does slow down traffic.

DECEMBER 1 ❧ CHRISTMAS

It is a mystery, attended to by a small sneering voice in my head. A child is born, God come to earth in human form. (*But – whispers the voice –I thought you said that God is always here.*) Angels announce this event in a sky filled with light. (*Angelic voices in this most rational of centuries? Huh.*) Three wise men deduce from watching a star that God will bring Godself into the human story. (*Astrology? Futurology? Huh, again.*)

But every year, just as I am wondering if I can even celebrate Christmas, something happens to that voice in my head. It may be when the newest baby in the congregation plays the child Jesus in the Christmas pageant, and I see the faces of the child's mother and father. (*They have seen God.*) Or the choir sings a song we hear only at this time of year, and the people sit hushed, willing it not to end. (*Oh. Of course. The lovely harmony of angels.*)

Three children dressed in bathrobes and cardboard crowns walk down the aisle toward a wobbly flashlight. As they giggle past, the flashlight becomes a star, the angels rejoice, and I am listening once more to an ancient story that is whole, complete, and absolutely necessary.

The scornful voice falls silent, and I hear only the language of love. It is the one language we could all speak. Whether we know it or not.

DECEMBER 2 ❧ THE SEASON OF DARKNESS

I wish there were no streetlights. I would like to see the stars. The world would be different, I think, if we stepped outside our doors and the whole sky was spread before us. We would remember awe.

DECEMBER 3 ❧ THE SEASON OF LIGHT

If we could have only quiet light. The moon. A ritual candle. When we have a candle-lit service the people sit in wonder, because most of our lives we sit by a glowing screen, or walk under a fierce streetlight, and we never, never know about the snow's reflection at night, or the way a single tiny flame can pierce the dark.

DECEMBER 4 ❧ GINGERBREAD PEOPLE

Eli was very little when he made his first gingerbread people. I assisted. He gave them as gifts to his mother and father, and when one of them took a huge bite, consuming an arm, he burst into desolate tears.

So God must feel.

DECEMBER 5 ✿ NANA AND ELI'S COOKIE RECIPE

This dough contains neither ginger nor molasses, so it is not, technically, gingerbread. But it is easy for children to work with and accepts so much rolling and re-rolling and cutting into shapes that we always use it to make people. Also, it is delicious.

½ cup butter
1 cup brown sugar
1 egg
1 teaspoon vanilla
1¾ cups flour
1 teaspoon baking powder
1½ teaspoons cinnamon
¾ teaspoon nutmeg
⅛ teaspoon cloves

Mix together flour, baking powder, and spices, and set aside. In another bowl, beat butter and sugar until smooth. Beat in egg and vanilla. Now stir in the flour mixture. Turn out onto a floured board or counter and knead with your hands until smooth. Shape into a ball, and roll out on floured surface to about ⅛-inch thickness. Cut into gingerbread people shapes and place on a greased cookie sheet. Bake at 350°F for about 10 minutes.

Let cool, on a rack or on the counter, and decorate. Eli and I find the tubes of coloured decorating icing from the store are easy for him to handle.

DECEMBER 6 ❧ THE MONTREAL MASSACRE

On this day, over 20 years ago, 14 women who had the audacity to study engineering at the École Polytechnique in Montreal were shot to death in their classroom by a mentally unstable man armed with a semi-automatic rifle. Immediately afterwards, Canada began work on a gun registry, supported by all political parties.

As I write, the registry is underway and working. Police like it. Most women's groups, aware of domestic violence issues, like it. Doctors, especially those emergency room doctors who see their share of bullet wounds, like it. So do nurses and paramedics. The registry is well used. Dropping it would save the government maybe $4 million a year, and cost us precious lives.

But not long ago I went to a rally in support of scrapping the registry. I guess I wanted to see how this could happen, how anyone could argue that we didn't need it. The speaker was Candace Hoeppner, then the Conservative Member of Parliament from Portage-Lisgar. She has carved out a peculiar niche for herself by supporting – as a woman – the stubborn irrationality of abolishing the gun registry. Hers is the party that bills itself as tough on crime but won't keep track of the rifles and shotguns that in 2008 accounted for almost three-quarters of all spousal homicides in Canada.

It is likely that, by the time you read this, the gun registry will be gone. I wish that women would stick together and remember their own: the 14 bright young women, the 14 grieving mothers whose beautiful daughters died from a gun in the hands of one who should never have been allowed a weapon.

DECEMBER 7 ❦ PRAYER FOR A CHRISTMAS PAGEANT

God of ice and sun,
Thank you for this Christmas story.
Thank you for allowing us to enter it with song and costume.
Thank you for the innkeeper, who teaches us to seek homes for those who have none.
Thank you for the sheep and cows and donkey, who teach us that God loves all earth's creatures.
Thank you for the exaltation of angels, the wonder of shepherds, the fierce science of the three kings. May they guide our own joy and wonder and curiosity.
Thank you for the fierce determination of Mary and Joseph to protect their little boy, who was, like every child, a miracle.
Please, God of snow and wind, please keep this story alight.
Please, God of story and song, preserve in us everything this brave

little boy came to teach:
Compassion for those who suffer,
Love for those who are hard to love,
Courage to challenge the powerful when they do wrong,
And the joy of one who lived in deepest friendship all his days.
Amen.

DECEMBER 8 ❧ THIS OLD CHURCH

My century-old church is lovely in December when its lavish stretches of old oak reflect candle flame. But the faith it was built to shelter in 1904 was vastly different from the one my friends and I wrestle with each week.

Our ancestors in faith looked up confidently towards heaven. So the English Gothic windows curve to a sharp upward peak. A similar motif is found on panels and furniture. The ceiling of the sanctuary is severely angular in height, also leading the eye upward. Even the arduous flight of stairs that move us up and up into worship assures us that the proper focus of our lives is skyward.

Strangely enough, it still works. The stained glass my ancestors filled with lilies and the balcony carved with stylized roses serve my faith, even though I am focused more on earth than heaven. A painting by Manitoulin artist Bebaminojmat (Leland Bell) dominates the front of the sanctuary. "The circle is central to our tradition," he says.

The gracefully curved pews form a circle of worship, the light pours in from four directions, and the Celtic cross is intersected by a circle – these all blend First Nations spirituality with Presbyterian consciousness to make a new faith.

At Christmas we are awed by God's majesty. But we also cling to the human shelter offered by the warm dark wood of our sanctuary ceiling. They say it was built by migrating shipwrights. It looks like my canoe. We could use this ceiling as an ark to save us here on earth.

DECEMBER 9 ❦ THE STAR

This month my friend Christel will do an astrological chart of my stars. She understands stars to be important. And so do I.

Christel's guide to the coming year is generally pretty accurate. Neither she nor I think the stars actually cause the incidents of the coming year, any more than a thermometer causes winter. But we agree with Richard Tarnas, who wrote in *Cosmos and Psyche* that "the human intelligence in all its creative brilliance is ultimately the cosmos's intelligence expressing *its* creative brilliance."

In other word, there's some connection. That is why I sing about the Three Wise Men, three astrologers, with delight.

Also, I am in favour of dark sky reserves where you can see the stars, and shielded, downward-facing street lights, and less, oh, please, less of the sheer extravagance of glowing office towers in the middle of the night.

Star of wonder.

DECEMBER 10 ❧ THE TREE

The Druids hung evergreen boughs at their doorways to keep away wicked spirits. Celts and Scandinavians and Germans brought in green boughs to reassure themselves that spring would come.

For me, the Christmas tree honours the boreal forest, the muskeg-laden, black spruce-crowded, granite-studded planetary lungs of our part of the world. For me, it symbolizes God's affection and respect for trees. I hang it with ornaments to domesticate its beauty, and to apologize for allowing it to be cut down.

DECEMBER 11 ❧ THE BABY

When a baby appears in your dream, pay attention. Something new wishes to be born in you. Something innocent and full of potential, something sacred that could change your world.

It's good to note which of your many selves is holding the child. (Yes, you do have many people within you: an old man, a mother, a wife, a queen… That's why Jungian analysts won't do group therapy. They are already dealing with so many voices.)

If your dream-child is in the hands of a wicked witch or a corrupt king like Herod, you might wish to get to know your own inner witch or tyrant. Perhaps they have something to teach you. Sometimes brutal dream-selves turn into benign fairy godmothers, when addressed. They want attention, and to be allowed out of the shadow.

Look carefully at the baby's setting, if it is clear. If the child seems impoverished, like another baby we hear a lot about this time of year, the dream might be attempting compensation for a life too rich in the wrong things, or unconcerned with the vulnerable.

There's a lot of ways to look at a baby. Especially if he or she is found in song or dream at Christmastime.

DECEMBER 12 ❧ SONGS

I used to sing in the choir. I loved it.

Now, on Sunday, I sit in the pew and listen (although we are allowed to sing sometimes too). And I love this too, the way each singing of a anthem adds more meaning, as if each song had a veil to be pulled aside a little at a time; as if the tune allowed the words to drift slowly, slowly, into my heart.

Listening like this without comment I hear things in a deeper way. I listen to the sermon and the scripture and the prayers of the people. None of these invite my spoken response, so I am free to rest in the meaning without debate, free to believe that I am loved.

Perhaps it would be good if the world had more times when we could just listen quietly and think, and then sing a little with our friends.

DECEMBER 13 ❧ ANGELS

I try to picture the heavenly host we hear about at this time of year, the angels who appeared, singing and lighting up the sky.

Would they be visible above the streetlights? Would we hear them above the traffic? Would a jetliner blow through the winged throng, startling the passengers and causing the pilots to contact air traffic control?

It's such a question. Is the world too sophisticated, now, for God? What if God rests securely only in the hearts of those who believe in the Bible literally and fundamentally, people who would consider my affection for pagan goddesses and sacred wells and springs to be reprehensible?

I hope not. We need God more than ever. We need to believe that each human has a sacred core that we respect in one another. We need the universe to have a soul. Without a soul, Earth herself is mechanical and dead and only fit for plunder.

Elders know about souls and singing angels and the God who is glory in the highest. We mustn't forget to pass this knowledge on.

DECEMBER 14 ❧ GOD OF WARMTH

The Scots prayed to bless the harvest and the birth of the child and the making of beer.

For a long time, in our determinedly secular world, I prayed only when I was overwhelmed by fear. But I am getting better. Next spring I will tuck transplants into the ground with a prayer of thanks and a whisper to grow well. Each night, we pray our thanks for dinner. Soon we'll get around to the other meals. When my children leave after a visit, I offer silently a *lorica*, a prayer of protection for their safe arrival home.

Oh, yes, I pray when I am cold with anxiety, as always. Often, warmth follows, and a whisper of peace.

DECEMBER 15 ❧ THE SANCTUARY

Sacred space between the worlds
Where Heaven and Earth encircle one another
And God and God's beloved clap their hands.
Sacred space between these walls
Where hands, God-given, carve a prayer in wood
And art and music whisper Alleluia.

DECEMBER 16 ❧ THE NEWSPAPER

I know that print editions of newspapers are going to disappear. I know the whole publishing industry is in flux. But I do love my daily newspaper, print edition. We elders need to know what is happening so we can write letters to the editor, online.

And I have lovely chats with our delivery person in the summer, when I am working in the front garden and he is delivering the paper in his very old car (older than ours) with his blue-eyed husky guarding the pile of papers in the back seat.

However, it's winter. Some days our newspaper does not arrive. Or maybe it has landed somewhere on the driveway or in a snowbank. I get my coat and my boots on and I go out, several times, wondering if my paper is just not here yet or if it has disappeared under falling snow. Could that depression in the snowbank be my paper?

Or is it maybe under the car in the driveway? My neighbours must be amused at my habit of emerging several times each morning to peer under the car. (Leaking oil? Kittens? Dementia?)

We elders cling to old-fashioned things, like the daily news in print, on paper, delivered to the house, and letters to the editor, and clippings stuffed into paper envelopes and sent to friends with our own handwriting scrawled across the top. "Can you believe this?!!" we write.

I want to enjoy this life until it is over.

DECEMBER 17 ❧ WHAT GOOD IS A BUILDING?

Twenty or so years ago our sanctuary was home to a host of people bewildered by the loss of 14 young women in Montreal – women they did not know but grieved for deeply. Almost a decade later, on September 11, 2001, the doors of our church, like many others, kept opening all day with people coming in. Many were in a panic as they waited to hear from loved ones in New York. Others just needed a place to pray.

Vigil services were held.

This is a sacred space for those who have none, where songs are sung for those who cannot believe. It is a sanctuary.

DECEMBER 18 ❧ CHRISTMAS PRAYER

I am your story, Storytelling God. I bring the stories of this year to you for blessing, the times I have been brave, and times I ran away.

You are the journey, God of wanderers. I bring the journeys of this year for blessing, the times I have been sad, and the times I have been wrapped in joyous wonder.

I am a shepherd, God of many flocks. To you I bring the ones I love for blessing, in the times when I am anxious, and the times when I delight.

You are the song, God of angels. To you, I bring my songs of hope for blessing, for the times when I am mute, and the times when I can sing. Amen.

DECEMBER 19 ❧ THE SUPER MARKET

Holiday grocery shopping is at hand. The children are coming. I must make everything they like. The house must smell of coffee and cinnamon and apples.

I go to the supermarket and push my overloaded trolley among all the other laden trolleys and see my friends, their grown children with them. We shout with delight and giggle at the grandbabies tucked amongst the fresh fish and green peppers and chocolate.

I remember to thank the manager for putting fair trade coffee on the shelf. I choose tomatoes and cheese with all the expertise of my 67 years. I do not care, this shopping trip, about the cost of things.

This supermarket is – in one way – like the summer farmers' market.

Because the farmers' market, says writer Michael Pollan, is where "someone buying food...may be acting not just as a consumer but also as a neighbor, a citizen, a parent, a cook. In many cities and towns, farmers' markets have taken on (and not for the first time) the function of a lively new public square."

Of course, I have a long, long way to go. The food movement, as Pollan articulates it, suggests that – instead of considering only price and quality – "ethical and political values should inform our buying decisions, and that we'll get more satisfaction from our eating when they do."

The fair trade coffee is a start, a sign of what could come. The shrieks of delight along the aisles, the visiting, the recipes for slow cooked foods in hand – we could build on this. We could begin here. We could pay a few cents more for our tomatoes and bananas in order to seek just payment for produce pickers everywhere. We could thank the manager for stocking local free-range eggs, and buy them.

We could pay a little more without complaint, as we tend to do at Christmas. And it would be a *super* market.

DECEMBER 20 ❧ REFUGEES: A CHRISTMAS STORY

When King Herod heard rumours of a new King born in his area, he made his brutal decision: Kill all the newborn boys, in case one of them should grow up to supplant him.

So the three astrologers who had been led by a star to the new god-child went home by another way, ignoring Herod's invitation to visit. And the little holy family, warned of Herod's intentions in Joseph's dream, picked off the hayseeds still clinging from the manger and fled to Egypt.

Canada has been the Egypt for many fleeing people for so long. We must not forget. We must not become the new Herods.

DECEMBER 21 ❦ MOTHER

Surely this is the holiest place in the universe, this small room with a dim light shielded by a cracked and peeling lampshade. The lamp came from the chaplain as a kind alternative to the harsh fluorescent light.

The friends are kind. The caregivers, coming and going, are as kind to her as if she were a beautiful young girl, not a woman well into her nineties with no eyesight nor very much hearing.

Outside the snow falls, along with darkness. Death is as much a miracle as birth. I know this now.

DECEMBER 22 ❦ THE GIFT

About thirty years ago I decided I would teach an adult education course in creative writing at the local community college. I had published exactly one book and attended exactly one workshop, which I thought would give me some ideas. I was quite young.

For some reason I was hired. My students were gracious. Most were women, a few of them teachers who instinctively brought their knowledge to the table. They all wanted to learn. We figured out together how to make it work.

Because most of what I had in print were personal essays, and because many of them were writing poems, also personal, we got to know each other well. One evening a woman read aloud her essay about being a lesbian. The term "gay" wasn't as much in the public lexicon as it is now.

The room was extremely quiet. I was a little dazed. I had never experienced anyone coming out before, particularly not a gentle middle-aged woman. I am not sure – remember, this was thirty years ago – that any of us knew the term "coming out."

When she was finished, the class went to work as always. They critiqued her piece of prose by all our usual criteria, as if she had been writing about refinishing furniture or her trip to Japan. They thanked her. I thanked her. We always thanked participants after a reading, because any piece of writing makes you vulnerable.

I taught the class for 13 more years. The women stuck to one another like glue. There was never any trouble filling the class; most of them came back every year. When I stopped teaching they formed a writers' club and carried on. They raised money for the Writers Development Trust. Many of them were published. One received numerous awards. They were a literary whirlwind. I think one factor was that quiet, graceful reading on a then-forbidden subject. It was a gift of trust.

We learned that writing well takes courage.

DECEMBER 23 ❧ OLD AND YOUNG TOGETHER

This is the season when elders and youngsters find each other. They collude at gifts for the generation in the middle. They share roles in the Christmas pageant. They bake together, if they are fortunate. They talk.

This is how things should be. Because old and young need to talk.

Increasingly, in Canada, it is the elders who remember how our fragile democracy once cared for everyone equally. It was not perfect, but we thought once, as a country, that there was such a thing as the common good. This notion is under fierce assault.

So I will talk. I will tell Eli how his great-grandma Margaret never missed a vote until she died. When she could no longer see, she would accompany me into the polling booth and I would cast her ballot under her whispered direction. I will tell him how his Baba, Jim, flew to South Africa to monitor their very first free election. Eli will laugh with me when he hears how – while other countries equipped their representatives with flak jackets – a tall Mountie in Pietermaritzburg gave his Baba a first-aid kit.

I will tell him how I bought my first grown-up briefcase when I came back from Central America and our little delegation was invited to meet then-Secretary of State for External Affairs, Joe Clark. When Eli is older, I will explain that we described the plight of internal refugees in El Salvador, and that Clark listened closely, with compassion, although he made no mention of my shiny briefcase.

We will talk. I will tell my grandson about those days when Canada cared.

DECEMBER 24 ❧ MOTHER EARTH

If one we love is ill, we do not desert her. We accompany, we wait, we sit with her pain, we do what we can to bring about her healing.

In the same way, our love does not change with the shifting fates of our Mother Earth. We sit with the pain of toxic tailing ponds and salty streets. We bless the wetlands, over and over, because they clean the water before it hits the lake and we need them to be healthy and complex and full of rich life as never before.

We try to live lightly and gracefully and lovingly with God's aching earth.

DECEMBER 25 ❧ CHRISTMAS DINNER

Our lives are stitched together by this feast, so beloved, so jammed with family-and-friends.

For many years we were 25 or so for Christmas dinner, crowding into the kitchen and filling extra tables pressed into service in the living room and dining room and sun porch, all disguised with white cloths.

I love to dress up tables.

The old ones crowd here with us, even though they're gone. The chair to the right of the fireplace was where my mother sat every Christmas afternoon, shouting orders to the kitchen where I found so much work to do I couldn't hear. Joy used to sit with her, of Joy-and-Ivan, our loved friends who always brought the turkey, splendidly tender, and Ivan's thin, old, lethal carving knife which he wielded with vast elder experience.

We still laugh over the time the bowl of whipped cream for the pumpkin pies slipped out of Cliff's hands and flew the length of the kitchen, leaving gobs of white all the way. And I remember the year I thought I would simplify this feast by omitting the Christmas crackers with their silly paper hats that always break apart when you put them on.

"Donna, WHERE ARE THE CRACKERS?" my mother demanded fiercely, and I rummaged around in the basement until I found some.

The old ones are present in our memories, vivid on this day. At the latest Christmas dinner, table set and dishes steaming, again I thought I would simplify the meal and not have crackers.

"Nana, where are the crackers?" my grandson whispered to me, looking puzzled.

Soon we were all wearing big grins and silly, tattered paper hats.

DECEMBER 26 ❧ BOXING DAY

E ven as elder women we don't forget the bliss of Boxing Day. The great feast is over and done but the leftovers richly remain. There will be no cooking today, just re-warming the abundance.

I will wear my pajamas all day, even under my snow gear to go sliding.

I will touch gifts received and marvel at the love of others.

And there will be a fire in the fireplace, all day.

DECEMBER 27 ❧ TO THE FIRE-BUILDER

When I am dying I would like a fire,
smoke curling in my nose

There, just there, at the end of my bed,
just off the green institutional spread –
That won't do.
I shall have to die at home
in your arms
knowing that time finally
caught us and pummeled us and won.
But the fire –
Time can't defeat it, the flames burn out in their own time
And leave some warmth behind that lasts awhile.

DECEMBER 28 ❧ MESSAGES

Jim and I were away from home. There was a bit of a family crisis and we were there to be supportive. But I was very anxious.

When I checked messages back on our home phone, though, my friend Diana had left a long one.

Diana is psychic – there, I have said it – and I have learned to trust her abilities. She had had a vision, she explained, of my mother. Diana had been working outside when she saw my mother "wearing a red dress and looking radiant."

"I just felt this must be a message for you," said Diana, who knew absolutely nothing of our private dilemma. "Your mother was so happy and she said 'Don't worry.' And there was someone else there with her, someone named Tattie or Tatiana..."

My mother's youngest sister was named Catherine, but my brother as a child had re-named her Tattie. She had died some years ago. Diana knew nothing of her.

Our culture is not at ease with this kind of event. But I am. Diana and I have known each other for a long time, and we have learned to tell each other this kind of story. We know what a vision is, and we respect it.

This one helped me. I stopped worrying. We got through the crisis.

We should not banish psychics from this century. We still need them.

DECEMBER 29 ❧ LIGHT

One year, our Jewish grandson was visiting at Hanukkah. We had no *Hanukkiya* (the nine-candled candelabra) so we made one from bright-coloured Lego, and fastened birthday candles to it, and put it in the window. We lit a candle every day of Hanukkah.

Eli was too little to understand the story of how the temple was restored to Jewish hands and the holy lamp re-lit, but we told it to each other anyway. The story tells that it was important that the flame not go out. There was only enough olive oil for one night, but it burned for eight nights until new oil could be pressed. Unless there is danger of persecution, *hanukkiyas* are placed in windows to announce this miracle widely.

Hannukuh is called the Festival of Lights. There are presents, and latkes. It most often falls in December, when Eli enjoys more presents, and turkey.

The reason for the latkes is the oil in which they cook, a reminder of the miracle of the holy light. I know no special reason for the turkey.

December is a month for miracles and gifts.

DECEMBER 30 ❧ THE JOY OF COLD

I love cold the way some people love heat. It began when I was in menopause. (Yes, for those readers still in it, or yet to be surprised by it, menopause does end. Eventually.)

At that time it was clear to me that I could heat the nation if someone could just figure out how to harness the raw energy I was producing. Other elder women have told me they felt the same.

The sense of being rescued by winter remains with me. Although I am a pushover for almost anything my family wants that is in my capacity to deliver, I do not budge when it comes to the temperature of our house.

It is frigid.

There are warm comforters all over the place, so those who wish to sit and chat can huddle in them. Sweaters are readily available. And did I mention that I like a fire in the fireplace?

I admit I have been known to make a warm and comforting stew on the coldest days, just so I can turn the oven on. But for the most part, the colder it is, the happier I am.

My heat-producing sisters and I are in solidarity with the polar bear. We are not pleased by global warming.

DECEMBER 31 ❧ RESOLUTIONS

This is a time for partying or prayer, whichever you prefer. It is a time to consider who we are, and what we must do with the rest of our lives. It is a time to call upon the ancestors for guidance.

You can party first, if you like. It is very important to wish a Happy New Year to as many people as you can, and mean it.

But today, or tomorrow, or this coming week, you must consider carefully who you are, and what you can do with your remaining life that will be good. You must try to do what elders do – in your own town, your own country.

As for me, I will keep my country in my heart; the Canada that should be saved, the one that cared for the common good. (I went to university because we had equalization grants for Northern Ontario students, and I received the bursaries assembled for students who hadn't the funding to attend otherwise.)

I will keep in my heart the memory of intelligent debate at many national gatherings. (I watched our Church's General Council, for one instance, when the youth – eloquently speaking – persuaded their elders that yes, this church should and could support gay marriage.) Canadians – and Americans and Australians and others – are all capable of such debate.

I will tell the young ones about this, in print and in person, for the rest of my life. They need to know that it is necessary to care, respectfully, for one another. This is how our lovely, battered, fragile country works.

❧ ENDNOTES

February 6   [1] From *A New Creed*. The United Church of Canada Service Book. (The Committee on Worship: The United Church of Canada, 1969), 310.

March 4   [2] The United Church Archives: Correspondence, V. Cheung, South China.

March 13   [3] Transition Towns is the term for a growing international movement aimed at enabling local communities to become more resilient in the face of climate change, peak oil, and global financial crises. "Transitioning" out of our dependence on fossil fuels is an important consideration.

May 14   [4] Moore, C. J., ed., *Carmina Gaedelica Hymns and Incantations Collected in the Highlands and Islands of Scotland in the Last Century by Alexander Carmichael* (Lindisfarne Books, 1992) p. 93

October 7   [5] From a speech delivered at a Ten Days for Global Justice seminar, Toronto, Canada, 1998.

❧ BIBLIOGRAPHY

It would be difficult to list all the titles that have influenced this book. However, the following are either quoted in the text, or form a useful background to some passages.

Armstrong, Karen. *The Great Transformation: The Beginning of Our Religious Traditions* (Toronto: Knopf Canada, 2007).

Berger, Warren. *Glimmer: How Design Can Transform Your Life, Your Business, and Maybe Even the World* (Toronto: Random House of Canada, 2009).

Carmichael, Alexander. *Carmina Gadelica: Hymns & Incantations from the Gaelic* (Gt. Barrington MA: Lindisfarne Books, 1992).

Cowan, Tom. *Fire in the Head: Shamanism and the Celtic Spirit* (New York: HarperCollins Publishers, 1993).

Crossan, John Dominic. *The Historical Jesus: The Life of a Mediterranean Jewish Peasant* (New York: HarperCollins Publishers, 1991).

Diamond, Jared. *Collapse: How Societies Choose to Fail or Succeed* (New York: Viking, 2005).

Dyer, Gwynne. *Future: Tense: The Coming World Order* (Toronto: McLelland & Stewart, 2004).

Frye, Northrop. *The Educated Imagination* (Toronto: CBC Publications, 1963).

Hall, James A. *Jungian Dream Interpretation: A Handbook of Theory and Practice* (Toronto: Inner City Books, 1983).

Hamilton, Garry. *Super Species: The Creatures That Will Dominate the Planet* (Richmond Hill: Firefly, 2010).

King, Thomas. *The Truth about Stories: A Native Narrative* (Toronto: Anansi, 2003).

Lawrence-Lightfoot, S. *The Third Chapter: Passion, Risk, and Adventure in the 25 Years After 50* (New York: Farrar, Straus and Giroux, 2009).

McDonald, Marci. *The Armageddon Factor: The Rise of Christian Nationalism in Canada.* (Toronto: Random House of Canada, 2010).

McKibben, Bill. *Eaarth: Making a Life on a Tough New Planet* (Toronto: Knopf Canada, 2010).

Mending The World: An Ecumenical Vision for Healing and Reconciliation (Toronto: The United Church of Canada, 1997).

Mitchell, Alanna. *Sea Sick: The Global Ocean in Crisis* (Toronto: McClelland & Stewart, 2009).

Mogel, Wendy. *The Blessing of a Skinned Knee: Using Jewish Teachings to Raise Self-Reliant Children* (New York: Penguin Books, 2001).

Pollan, Michael. *In Defense of Food: An Eater's Manifesto* (New York: Penguin Press, 2008).

Saul, John Ralston. *A Fair Country: Telling Truths about Canada* (Toronto: Viking Canada, 2008).

Skibsrud, Johanna. *The Sentimentalists.* (Vancouver: D&M Publishers Inc., 2010).

Soelle, Dorothee. *The Strength of the Weak: Toward a Christian Feminist Identity.* (Philadelphia: The Westminster Press, 1984).

Tarnas, Richard. *Cosmos and Psyche: Intimations of a New World View.* (New York: Viking, 2006).

Websites
Transition Towns
http://www.transitionnetwork.org/

Imagine Sudbury
http://imaginesudbury.com/

Friends of Sweetman's Garden
http://www.sweetmansgarden.com/

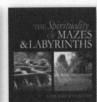

ok jackets and full-colour images
llness & beauty of life.

  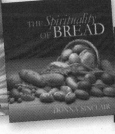

**he Spirituality
f Music**
ohn Bird

**The Spirituality
of Art**
Lois Huey-Heck
and Jim Kalnin

**The Spirituality
of Gardening**
Donna Sinclair

**The Spirituality
of Bread**
Donna Sinclair

**The Spirituality
of Wine**
Tom Harpur

"Without bread and all it symbolizes for humanity at the physical level, the life of the body would be impossible. Without the "bread" of spiritual sustenance, the human soul lies empty and inert. Thus, it is no accident that both in the religion of ancient Egypt and in the Jesus Story the theme of bread – of bread being multiplied – lies at the heart of the sacred myth. Bethlehem, for example, means "the house of bread." In The Spirituality of Bread, *Donna Sinclair has richly explored and blessed for her readers these profoundly universal truths.*

– TOM HARPUR, BESTSELLING AUTHOR OF MANY BOOKS INCLUDING
THE SPIRITUALITY OF WINE AND *THE PAGAN CHRIST*